The Desktop Color
B O O K

A Verbum Guide
by Michael Gosney and Linnea Dayton

MIS:
PRESS

A Subsidiary of
Henry Holt and Co., Inc.

Project Producer: Michael Gosney
Chief Writer/Editor: Linnea Dayton
Art Director: John Odam
Editor/Writer: Jackie Estrada
Gallery Editors: Michael Gosney and Aleta Reese
Production: Betsy Kopshina and Melea Morris
(with thanks to Jill Davis, Danielle Foster,
Richard Carter and Ed Roxburgh)
Illustrations: John Odam and artists as listed on page vi
Glossary: Steven Rosenthal
Administrative Management: Leslie Banach
Inspiration: Bob Angus

Cover design and illustration: John Odam

Project Manager: Debra Williams Cauley
Managing Editor: Cary Sullivan
Technical Editors: Paul Ramirez,
Giovanni Fortezza and Megan Pugh
Copy Editors: Shari Chappell and Jack Donner

The Desktop Color Book is a Verbum, Inc. production. For a free catalog of Verbum books and CD-ROMs on digital creativity, contact: Verbum, P.O. Box 189, Cardiff, CA 92007, tel 619-944-9977, fax 619-944-9995, net pubinfo@verbum.com.

MIS:Press books are available at special discounts for bulk purchases for sales promotions, premiums, fund-raising, or educational use. Special editions or book excerpts can also be created to specification. For details contact:
Special Sales Director
MIS:Press
a subsidiary of Henry Holt and Company, Inc.
115 West 18th Street
New York, New York 10011
First edition published by Verbum Books, 1992
Second edition published by M&T Books/MIS:PRESS, 1994

Printed in the United States of America

10 9 8 7 6 5 4 3 2 1

Library of Congress Cataloging-in-Publication Data
Gosney, Michael, 1954–
   The Desktop Color Book / Michael Gosney and Linnea Dayton,
   Includes index
   ISBN 1–55828-365-X : $19.95
   1. Desktop publishing, 2. Color computer graphics. L. Dayton
   Linnea, 1944-
   Z253, 53, 066   1994
94-34331
   666.2'2544536—dc20
                     CIP

Welcome to a User-Friendly Verbum Guide!

Welcome to the updated, expanded second edition of *The Desktop Color Book*. This compact volume guides you through the ins and outs of color publishing using today's powerful desktop computer systems. It provides an overview of color theory and practice as implemented on the desktop. It covers the basics of what color is and how to make the most of it with digital design and production tools.

The book is designed to serve as a comprehensive and accurate—but not too

technical—guide to desktop color. It will appeal to people entering this field, and even to those who have no plans to enter it but are curious about one of the major technical revolutions of our time.

For those who already work in desktop publishing or digital prepress *The Desktop Color Book* is designed to fill in the gaps in their knowledge of the overall design-to-publication process, and to provide some specific tips for achieving success. The book progresses from the basics of color and the computer through the processes of bringing raw material for artwork into the computer, creating the artwork itself and getting the finished art out of the computer and onto the printed page.

We've enjoyed bringing this fairly complex subject into a friendly format—and we hope it inspires and facilitates the effective use of color in your work.

An Overview

Chapter 1 provides background for the discussion of color on the desktop by first defining color, then discussing the models and terminology we use to describe it, and finally presenting some tips for choosing color schemes.

Chapter 2 gives a brief rundown of the kinds of computer equipment currently used to work with color on the desktop. To make it easier to understand how desktop color works, this chapter also tells how the computer encodes and displays color, and gives an overview of how painting, photo editing, drawing, 3D and page layout programs work.

Chapter 3 describes the various options for input and storage of computer artwork, including drawing or painting with handheld input devices, scanning images, using Photo CD scans and grabbing video frames. This chapter also introduces the topic of resolution—the amount of detail that's recorded, displayed or printed in an image—and shows how scanning resolution, display resolution and printing resolution are related. A discussion of the choices available for efficient, reliable storage of graphics files, which can easily get very large, completes this chapter.

Chapters 4 and 5 discuss the kinds of software—object-oriented PostScript illustration and continuous-tone painting and image-manipulation programs—most often used to create artwork, describing how these kinds of programs work and providing some specific tips and techniques.

Chapter 6 offers a discussion of output options, with an emphasis on printing artwork on paper, but also with a discussion of output for multimedia. It includes advice for getting predictable color from desktop output and for choosing and working with the imagesetting service bureaus that produce color-separated film from desktop files.

Chapter 7, The Verbum Gallery, is a showcase of color illustrations from leading commercial illustrators and fine artists working with desktop color tools.

Finally, the Desktop Color Glosssary defines the essential terms.

CONTENTS

Illustration Credits and Production Notes

Chapter 1
Janet Ashford chapter opening
John Odam 1–19

Chapter 2
Janet Ashford 11, 13, 21
Jack Davis chapter opening
Jill Davis 14
Betsy Kopshina 16
John Odam 1–10, 12
Russel Riben 15

Chapter 3
Janet Ashford 1–2, sidebar p. 25, 4–5, 7, 10–12
Betsy Kopshina 3
Mark Landman chapter opening
John Odam 6, 8, 9

Chapter 4
Janet Ashford 1–10, 14, 16–18, 20–21, 24–28, 30–31
Linnea Dayton 29
Tom Gould 11
Betsy Kopshina 19
Steve Musgrove 6
John Odam 12–13, 22–23
David Smith chapter opening, 15

Chapter 5
Janet Ashford 3–11, 15–16, 19–21, 24–27
Linnea Dayton 17
Betsy Kopshina 13–14,18
Bert Monroy 22–23
John Odam chapter opening, 2
Norbert Schultz 12
Sharon Steuer 1

Chapter 6
Janet Ashford 4, 7,10
Jack Davis 11
Jill Davis 3, 5
Louis Fishauf chapter opening
John Odam 1–2, 8–9

The Desktop Color Book was designed and produced with PageMaker 5.0 on Macintosh IIcx and Quadra 800 computer systems. Scanned images were captured using UMAX UC360 and LaCie Silverscanner flatbed scanners for reflective art and a Crossfield scanner for transparencies. Color separations were output at 150 lpi on a Agfa SelectSet 7000 imagesetter. The book was printed on a Hantscho press on 80# St. Lawrence Gloss stock with CMYK process inks.

Introduction: Where This Book and Its Subject Came From

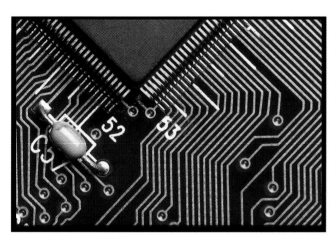

DESKTOP COLOR first poked its head out of primitive silicon wafers and clunky scanners back in the late 1970s. In the 80s, a wave of high-end dedicated computer systems for electronic publishing came and, for the most part, went. The origins of today's brave new world of color publishing date to the mid-80s when the Amiga computer dazzled us with animated color and we puzzled over the Mac's tiny, quite colorless, etch-a-sketch screen. But the Macintosh II, the fabled "Color Mac," with a brilliant high-resolution Sony monitor, armed with PostScript, proved to be the true seed of the desktop color paradigm. While the Amiga, a natural-born, multi-tasking animation engine with a natural penchant for video, went on to revolutionize video production with the Toaster and other breakthroughs, and the DOS-encumbered PC played endless catch-up but helped fuel the industry's fire with a voracious corporate market, the Macintosh captured the imagination of both engineers and artists, and innovations on both sides of the screen came rapid-fire. Graphic designers caught on to the tools. Propeller heads caught on to design. The computer press trumpeted the call, and a world of advanced digital communications known as "desktop publishing" emerged in a swirl of fast-evolving graphics-oriented system software, numerous inspired applications, the complete digitalization of the typography trade, clip media from every which way, desktop and handheld scanners, desktop printers, all made affordable by the vast numbers of the desktop "one person, one computer" market. Like video cameras, VCRs and other high-tech consumer products, the scale, rapid growth and competitiveness of the desktop color computers resulted in nearly overnight evolution of these advanced, inexpensive, truly amazing systems. The revolution was over, in a sense, within five years. By the beginning of the 1990s, the professions of graphic design, typography, camera services, color separation and printing had been transformed, their systems retooled or replaced, old crafts lost, new crafts learned.

WE HAD FUN participating in all this with the publication of our digital art journal *Verbum*, one of the first fully desktop-published magazines, and the first widely seen showcase of design and illustration by trail-blazing artists. *Verbum* was a feedback loop connecting the artists with the industry's engineers and product managers. Our events—the Imagine Exhibit of Personal Computer Art ('88–'89 in San Diego, Boston, San Francisco and Tokyo), the annual Digital Art Be-Ins in San Francisco—and others, along with our books—*Making Art on the Macintosh II, The Verbum Book of* 5-book series, *The Gray Book* and the *Step-By-Step Electronic Design* newsletter we created for Dynamic Graphics—all contributed to the evolution of these new crafts.

THE DESKTOP COLOR BOOK was born in 1992 over lunch with a friend who mentioned how his clients involved in the desktop color market had a hard time educating their customers, not to mention their own colleagues, on the confusing new world of digital color. A "user-friendly guide" was needed. We put our experience together with that of industry and user experts, and sold the first edition mostly through mail order and directly to companies such as Radius, Kodak, QMS and Pantone. Since the first edition was such a smashing critical success, we sought a publisher for an updated and expanded second edition. Enter M&T Books, now part of MIS: Press/Henry Holt and Company, former publisher of the Verbum Book series. The book is in a larger format with over twice as many pages, up-to-date information, glossary and last but not least, the Verbum Gallery of Digital Art. **WE HOPE YOU'VE FOUND THIS CASCADE OF ENTHUSIASM INSPIRING**. Go ahead, sit down in front of that crisp 20-inch monitor, pull up a Photo CD image in Photoshop, and filter it; hook up a graphics tablet and load up Painter; scan in a sketch and draw your dream house in FreeHand; print out the video grab of your sweetie on your little color printer. **TELL ME YOU'RE NOT ENTHUSIASTIC TOO!**

— *Michael Gosney*

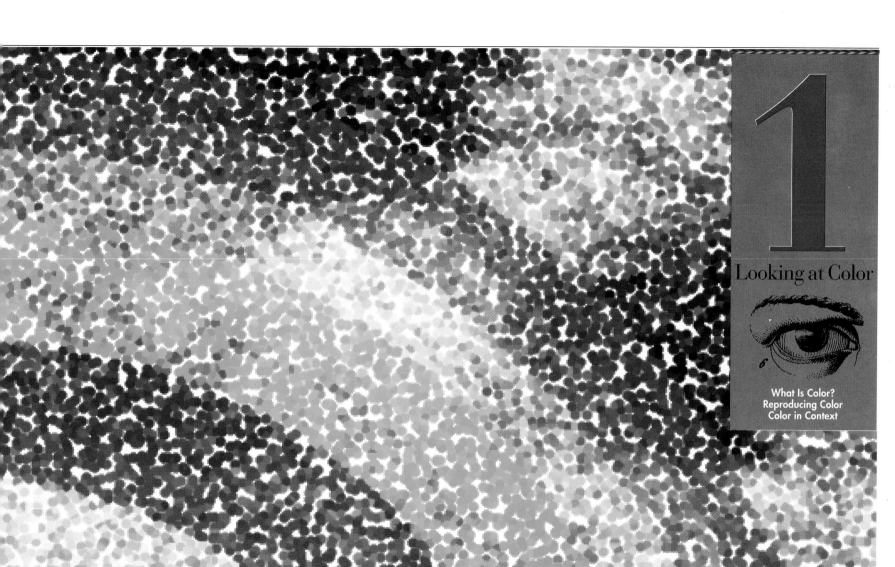

1

Looking at Color

What Is Color?
Reproducing Color
Color in Context

IF YOU ASKED a dozen people to "picture something red," it's likely that each of them would visualize a slightly different color—or even a range of colors, like the variety of reds on the skin of an apple. And yet, if you could show all parties what the others had visualized, most would probably agree that all the colors they had pictured would fall into a range they could call "red."

THE NEED FOR PRECISION Our perception of color is subjective, based on our visual system and our psychology. Furthermore, the everyday language of color is not precise. In a technical sense, though, we *can* describe color with great precision. In desktop color systems, we need to be able to characterize color precisely if we are to get predictable, repeatable results from scanners, from display monitors and on the printed page.

PROPERTIES OF COLOR Color is light—whether it comes directly from a light source, like the blue of a gas flame, or is reflected from an object, like the red of a stop sign. White light is made up of all colors. We can demonstrate this if we use a prism to divide a beam of white light into the spectrum of its component colors (1).

In scientific terms, color depends on three characteristics of light waves: length, amplitude and purity. Wavelength is the most important of the three factors in determining what we perceive as color; it's most closely related to the property of color called *hue* (2). Amplitude comes closest to color *brightness* (3), and purity determines what we call *saturation* (4).

MODELING COLOR To visualize how the three characteristics of light determine color, we can use a three-dimensional model based on the *CIE color space* (5). "CIE" stands for Commission International d'Eclairage, a standards committee that in 1931 established a system to define and measure color mathematically, so that all colors could be specified precisely. With a way to specify color and with instruments that can measure it (see "Measuring Color" on page 3), we have a basis for developing desktop systems that can reproduce color accurately.

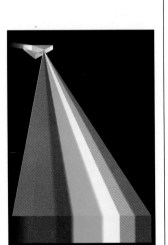

1 When white light passes through a prism, all the colors that compose it are spread out to form a *spectrum*. The spreading occurs because the prism bends the waves of the different colors of light in different amounts.

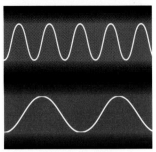

2 The wavelength of light determines hue. Wavelength is the distance from one peak of the wave to the next. Of the colors we can see, violet light has the shortest waves and red has the longest.

In Other Words...

Over the many years that people have been analyzing color, several schemes have been devised to describe it objectively, and so a number of terminologies have developed. These vocabularies have been carried over into the software used in desktop color work. It's easier to understand these color description systems if we know how they relate to one another, to the properties of light, and to the familiar, subjective names that people use for color in everyday conversation.

In the system that describes color in terms of **hue**, **saturation** and **lightness**, hue is specified by naming a color. When we add the terms **white**, **gray** and **black** to the color names, we complete a list of basic color descriptions. We can be more descriptive by adding adjectives derived from the color names themselves; for example, **greenish blue** or **reddish brown**.

Lightness (also referred to as **value**) is described by adjectives such as **light**, **medium** and **dark**; adding the adverb **very** to **light** or **dark** extends the range. **Brightness** also refers to essentially the same color property as lightness, with words like **dim** and **dazzling** representing the two extremes of the range.

Words used to describe saturation (which is also referred to as **chroma**) include **grayish**, **moderate**, **strong** and **vivid**. They indicate how much a color differs from a gray of the same lightness or brightness.

Although such language isn't precise, combining terms that describe the three properties of color communicates a familiar range of color possibilities. For example, **light grayish green** or **vivid medium yellow** help us designate a particular green or yellow range in a way that's generally familiar.

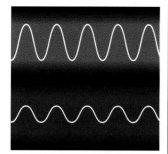

3 Amplitude, or the height of the wave from trough to peak, determines the brightness of a color. The greater the amplitude, the more energy in the wave and therefore the brighter the color.

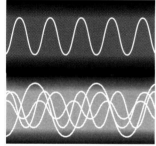

4 A pure, or completely saturated, color contains light of only one wavelength. As more wavelengths are added, the color becomes less distinct. When all visible wavelengths are mixed, the result is white light.

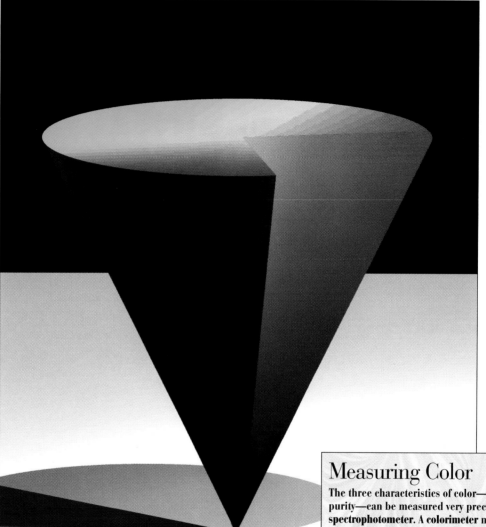

5 A color space model provides a three-dimensional way to visualize the relationship between hue, saturation and brightness. In this conical model, hue varies as you travel around the cone. Brightness varies as you travel up or down the cone, being greatest at the top and least at the bottom. Saturation varies as you travel inward or outward, with colors being least saturated in the center and most saturated at the outside surface. A color model like this is used as the basis for color pickers in many graphics programs.

Measuring Color

The three characteristics of color—wavelength, amplitude and purity—can be measured very precisely with an instrument called a **spectrophotometer**. **A colorimeter** measures the same characteristics but less precisely than the more expensive device. A **densitometer** takes less precise, or more approximate, readings of color. While a spectrophotometer or a colorimeter can come up with a number that will precisely locate a color in the CIE color space, for example, a densitometer cannot be as specific.

ONE OF OUR GOALS in using desktop color systems is to record—on the printed page, on videotape, on slide film or in some other medium—the colors that we see in nature, in a photo or in our mind's eye. Desktop color systems do this in two ways: through additive and subtractive color reproduction.

ADDITIVE COLOR In *additive color reproduction* three primary colors of light are combined in varying intensities to produce all the other colors. When the three primaries are added together, the result is white. This effect can be seen when the circles of light from colored spotlights overlap each other in a theatrical performance, for example (6).

Video monitors, like those used for television and for desktop color systems, reproduce colors by the additive method. When red, green and blue (RGB) phosphor coatings on the screen are bombarded by streams of electrons, they emit colored light. The amount of energy beamed at each phosphorescent dot determines how brightly lit it is and thus how intense its color is. The colors on the screen are determined by the mix of light from the red, green and blue dots. The individual dots can be seen with magnification (7).

SUBTRACTIVE COLOR In *subtractive color reproduction* color is produced when white light falls on a colored surface and is only partly reflected. A perfectly white surface reflects all wavelengths of light. A black surface absorbs all wavelengths, reflecting none. The yellow of a flower, for example, absorbs all light except a mix of wavelengths that we recognize as yellow; the reflected light, then, is what our eyes detect when we look at the flower. In contrast, green leaves absorb all wavelengths except those we perceive as green (8).

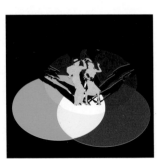

6 Additive color reproduction is used in video monitors, desktop scanners, film recorders and other color systems that are based on mixing light. The three primary colors, from which all others can be mixed, are red, green and blue; when mixed in equal parts, they make white. Other colors can be mixed by varying the amounts of the primaries.

7 On the screen of an RGB (red, green, blue) video display monitor, colors are formed as patterns of tiny red, green and blue dots. Each dot of each of the three colors can vary in brightness. The tiny dots are closely packed, so we see the color formed by the mixture of light from all three types of dots rather than seeing each dot individually.

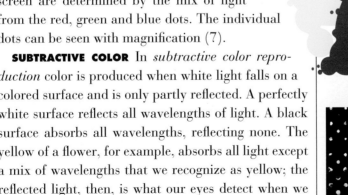

8 When light shines on a colored surface, some wavelengths are absorbed and some are reflected. The reflected light determines the color we see. In some cases, the light energy absorbed by the surface may be re-emitted as heat. That's why dark surfaces, which absorb more light energy than they reflect, tend to warm up more than light-colored surfaces made of similar materials.

9 The subtractive primaries of the printing process are cyan, magenta and yellow. Various mixtures of these three primaries form all the colors of the subtractive color reproduction system. If ink pigments were perfect, when mixed these three colors would form black, a "color" that absorbs all light and reflects none.

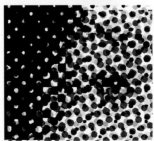

10 In the full-color printing process used to reproduce photos and blended colors on many printing presses, patterns of tiny dots are used to fool the eye into seeing a full range of colors. Unlike the video monitor, whose dots stay the same size but vary in brightness, these dots of subtractive primaries vary in size (as shown here) or in the number of dots per area. (Output dot patterning, or *screening*, is covered in Chapter 6.)

11 The range of colors that the human eye can see is larger than the range of colors that can be reproduced in the emulsions of photographic film and paper. The photographic gamut, in turn, is larger than the color gamut of the RGB video monitor, and the range of colors that can be printed with process inks is even smaller. This disparity in color gamuts is one potential source of frustration when we aim to match the vibrant colors of an original glossy photo or a brilliant on-screen display with inks printed on paper. (This diagram is, of course, only representational. Since it's printed with ink on paper, it couldn't really be designed to show the unprintable ranges of color that we can see or that we can capture with photographic film or display on an RGB monitor.)

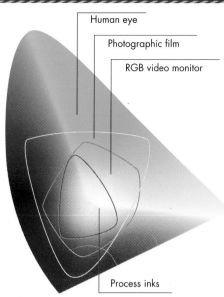

Human eye

Photographic film

RGB video monitor

Process inks

12 Custom-mixed inks such as those of the Pantone, Toyo and Focoltone systems can print some colors that cannot be achieved with dot patterns of cyan, magenta, yellow and black inks. Color swatch books show how these inks will look when printed. The Pantone Color Formula Guide 1000, for example, provides samples and ink-mixing formulas for more than 1000 colors that can be printed with solid coverage of Pantone color inks. Pantone also publishes process color guides that provide the closest process color matches for many of the solid Pantone colors.

In desktop color systems, and in the printing industry in general, the three primary colors of inks used in the subtractive color reproduction system are cyan, magenta and yellow (CMY) (9). However because printing ink pigments are not perfect, combining cyan, magenta and yellow does not make a clean, crisp-looking black. So black ink (the K of CMYK) is also applied. You can see how printed colors are made up of the subtractive primaries plus black if you use a loupe to examine a full-color photo printed in a magazine (10).

COLOR GAMUTS Whether we reproduce color by subtractive or by additive methods, we are limited in the colors we can make. Although RGB display monitors can produce many of the colors we see in the natural world, they cannot make all of them. And the color range, or *gamut*, that can be printed with CMYK inks is even more limited than the gamut of a display monitor (11).

CUSTOM COLOR One way to print a color that cannot be reproduced by varying the coverage of cyan, magenta, yellow and black inks is to mix an ink specifically for that color by combining pigments other than those of the four process printing inks. The inks of the Pantone Matching System, for example, are formulated to give consistent, reproducible colors (12).

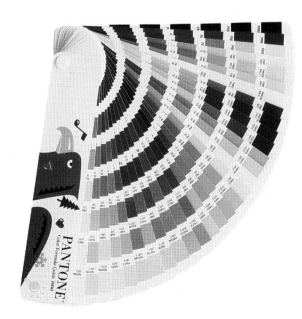

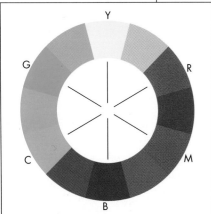

E ALL HAVE UNIQUELY personal responses to color. And yet our language shows us that we share some common psychological color perceptions. We speak of "seeing red" when we're angry, "feeling blue" when we're sad and "turning green with envy" or "purple with rage." Beyond such emotional responses, our visual systems respond physiologically to individual colors and to color interactions. To use colors effectively on the desktop (or elsewhere), it helps to know about how they are related and how they interact with one another. The dynamic color interactions that can be achieved with careful color selection can help make up for the limitations imposed by restricted color gamuts, such as those of printing inks.

COLOR WHEELS AND COLOR TRIANGLES A color wheel is a circular arrangement of hues that shows how primary colors (those from which all others can theoretically be mixed) and mixed colors are related to one another (13). If we look at the color wheel as a clock face, the three primary colors are spaced equally around the wheel, so that they would fall at 12 o'clock, 4 o'clock and 8 o'clock, for example. The mixture of any two primaries generates a *secondary color*, which occupies the position halfway between the two primaries, at 2, 6 or 10 o'clock in our example. *Intermediate colors* are mixtures of a secondary and one of its nearest primaries. More colors can be added to the wheel by continuing to mix colors from adjacent hues.

Any two colors that are directly opposite each other on the color wheel are *complements*. Mixed together equally, they theoretically form black or gray. Mixed in

13 A color wheel is a way of showing the compositional relationships among colors. Note the primary colors in the RGB version of the color wheel are the secondary colors in the CMY version and vice versa.

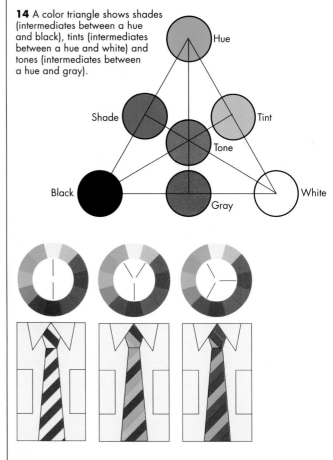

14 A color triangle shows shades (intermediates between a hue and black), tints (intermediates between a hue and white) and tones (intermediates between a hue and gray).

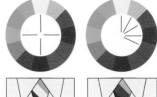

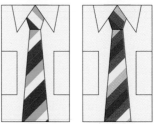

15 We can rely on certain kinds of relationships from the color wheel and color triangle to create pleasing combinations: for example, complements (top left), near complements (top center), triadic complements (top right), double complements (bottom left) and multiple complements (bottom right).

unequal parts, they tone down or desaturate each other.

The color wheel representation of colors does not deal with light and dark variations of a pure hue, but a color triangle can show these relationships (14).

PLEASING COLOR Color wheels and color triangles are helpful for assembling palettes of colors that go well together. While many colors can be made to blend harmoniously, especially if colors are used in relatively small areas, certain kinds of color combinations are generally accepted as pleasing (15):

- Complements (opposites on the color wheel)
- *Near complements* (or *split complements*)
- *Double complements* (two pairs of complementary colors)
- *Triads* (three equally spaced colors)
- *Multiple complements* (five adjacent colors on a wheel of primary, secondary and intermediate colors)
- In a color triangle, the colors along any straight line

COLOR INTERACTIONS Our observations of color in the real world, along with the peculiarities of the physiology of vision, make us see certain color effects that we might not expect. For example:

- Colors of different hues but the same intensity tend to "fight" each other for dominance in our visual system (16).
- Brightness and value can affect the perception of size, distance or dimensionality (17).
- A difference in the brightness of one color can trick the eye into seeing other color brightness differences that are not based on physical changes in color composition (18).
- Even patches of color with the same hue, brightness and saturation can look like different colors, depending on what other colors surround them (19).

16 Using contrasting colors of equal brightness and saturation can set up a lively visual interaction that makes a pattern look dynamic. But the same dynamics can be a disaster if the goal is to set readable type.

17 More and less saturated versions of the same hue can shape an object by making it look like its surfaces are in different relationships to a light source (above). Also, because of our experience with viewing things at a distance, decreasing brightness and saturation can contribute to the illusion that one object is farther away than another (top right). In addition, objects that are colored with brighter or more saturated versions of the same hue often look bigger than their paler, less colorful counterparts (right).

18 The effect of color brightness can be seen when a gradation from dark to light is placed behind a color of medium brightness. At the right (dark) end of the gradation, the foreground color looks light in contrast. In the middle, the medium part of the gradation tends to get lost. The left (light) section of the gradation makes the foreground look darker.

19 When an intermediate between two colors is surrounded by either of the colors, the effect is to "dilute" the shared component. For example, a green formed of yellow and cyan looks yellower when placed on a cyan background and bluer when surrounded by yellow.

2

Desktop Tools
for Color

**Desktop Hardware
Computer Color
Color Graphics Software
Palettes and Pickers**

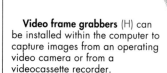

T O WORK WITH COLOR on the electronic desktop we need microcomputer-based *hardware* (1) along with graphics programs (*software*) to do the following jobs:

- Put information in, to compose an image.
- Display the image, so we can see it.
- Interact with the image to make changes to it.
- Store the image in intermediate or final form, so we don't have to start from scratch each time we turn on the computer.
- Reproduce the image in a form we can conveniently circulate to others—printed on paper, for example, or as a 35mm slide.

In addition, the hardware and software have to perform the calculations that are needed as these tasks are carried out, and they also have to manage the flow of information between the various parts of the system.

MANAGING DIGITAL INFORMATION Computers keep track of images—and for that matter all the other kinds of information they handle—digitally. That is, all the information that a computer processes exists in the form of numbers. We can think of the computer's central processing unit (or *CPU*) as the "brains" of the desktop hardware. It runs the system software that manages the "traffic" of computer operation, coordinating the input, storage and display of information, and the output. It also runs the graphics software we use, carrying out the arithmetic necessary to create or modify images. The CPU needs enough random access memory (or *RAM*) to keep track of both the graphics software and the image we are working on. It requires enough speed to complete graphics tasks quickly, so that delays don't interfere with the artist's ability to create. In general, working with color requires more CPU speed and more memory than working with black-and-white images; and the more realistic or wide-ranging the color, the more speed and memory it takes.

1 A **trackball** (A) moves an on-screen pointer by rotating a ball within a stationary base.

The **keyboard** (B) is ideal for setting type and for entering commands in graphics programs.

The **mouse** (C) is rolled around the desktop to position, select and move parts of graphic images.

Desktop computer systems can read information (such as stored photo images) from a **CD-ROM** (compact disc read-only memory) disc drive (D).

A **graphics tablet** (E) and **stylus** (F) can provide the feel of traditional drawing and painting tools. With the appropriate graphics software, they can vary the intensity or flow of the color on the computer according to the pressure applied to the stylus tip.

Scanners (G) are used to input photographic images and other source artwork. (Scanning is covered in Chapter 3.)

Video frame grabbers (H) can be installed within the computer to capture images from an operating video camera or from a videocassette recorder.

The **CPU** (I) manages the tasks the computer carries out. It can speed up these tasks by running faster (at a higher megahertz rating) or by "subcontracting" some operations to other CPU-like hardware called *coprocessors*. (For more about increasing speed in desktop computers, see "Maximizing Speed" on page 11.)

The **monitor** (J) displays the *interfaces* of graphics software, through which the artist can choose and apply the functions the program uses to create and edit images.

Cables and **connectors** (K and L) link the parts of a desktop color system and provide a way to pass information from one component of the system to another.

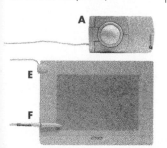

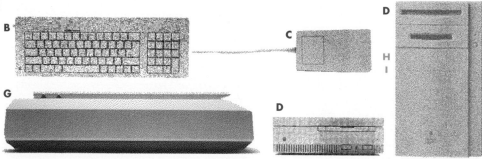

Floppy disks (M) are inexpensive and portable magnetic storage media, but they hold less information than other media, typically only 800 kilobytes (K) or 1.4 megabytes (MB).

Hard disk drives (N) typically used in desktop graphics systems can hold approximately 20 to 2000 times as much information as floppy disks, also on magnetic media. A hard disk drive can be built-in or attached to the CPU by cabling.

Optical disk drives (O) use laser technology (or lasers and magnetism) to record and store 128 MB to 1.3 GB of information on disks not much larger than floppies.

A **removable cartridge drive** (P) system provides a relatively large storage capacity (usually 44 or 88 MB per disk) on disks that are well-protected and small enough to be transported quite easily.

N

O

P

ENTERING AND CHANGING INFORMATION The desktop *input devices* we can use to import, create or modify color images include scanners, keyboards, mice, trackballs, graphics tablets, CD-ROM (compact disc read-only memory), digital cameras and frame grabbers for importing images from live video or videotape. These devices work with graphics programs that accept their input and use it to produce electronic artwork or photo images on screen, paper or film.

Desktop systems have been made compatible with the more complex input equipment traditionally used by color separation specialists. So high-end scans such as those from Scitex and Linotype-Hell systems can also be used on the desktop.

DISPLAYING THE IMAGE Display monitors vary in size and color capabilities, from small black-and-white formats to 8-bit or 24-bit color screens large enough to show an entire page or two-page spread at full size. (For information about the relationship between bits of data and the display of color, see "Computer Color" on page 12.)

STORING IMAGES Graphics files, like other computer data, can be stored on floppy disks, hard disks (fixed or removable), CD-ROM, optical disks or magnetic tape. Efficient storage requires adequate space for programs and graphics files, as well as quick access when the CPU calls for information from a stored file. Some graphics programs also use storage space as *virtual memory*. Virtual memory accepts the overflow when there isn't enough RAM available to hold an entire active graphics file. It stores parts of the file temporarily while the computer works on other parts.

PRINTING IMAGES Much of the artwork created on the electronic desktop is eventually output as high-resolution film negatives, paper prints, 35mm slides or CD-ROM. The relatively expensive imagesetters, color printers, slide makers and CD-ROM writers that produce this kind of output are usually found in imagesetting service bureaus, whose trained operators handle a high volume of this work. However, desktop systems require printers—typically laser printers and color thermal transfer or inkjet printers—for checking pages before they are sent to such a service bureau.

Maximizing Speed

Accelerator boards increase the power of desktop computers by increasing processing speed; accelerating screen response for routine operations like scrolling, resizing and color filling; and providing slots for additional memory (RAM), which allows many graphics programs to operate more efficiently. In addition, some accelerator boards are designed to carry out time-consuming functions for particular programs, leaving the CPU free for other tasks.

Digital audio tape (DAT) drives (Q) can be used to make back-up copies of graphics files. Although they can't retrieve the graphics information fast enough to be used for storage while the files are being worked on, they are ideal for *archiving* (safe, long-term storage) because a large amount of data can be packed into a very small volume. (CD-ROM storage, although not yet as inexpensive as DAT, is even more stable, and data retrieval is much quicker.)

A **laser printer** (R) prints images by using heat to fuse its dry ink (or *toner*) to the page to form black-and-white images according to the instructions provided to it by the computer's graphics software.

Desktop color printers (S) (thermal transfer, inkjet or dye sublimation) provide color prints for evaluating artwork and page layouts during the design process. These printers can also produce final pages suitable for some specialized uses. (For more about desktop color printers, see page 64.)

Q

R

S

A PICTURE ON A COMPUTER SCREEN looks to us like a drawing, a painting, a photograph or a collage. But the computer sees the image as a *data file*, or a collection of information. Computers handle information by turning tiny electronic switches OFF or ON. For example, each of the dot positions (or *pixels*, short for *picture elements*) on a computer monitor's screen has one or more of these switches associated with it. The number of switches used to describe the color of each pixel depends on how detailed, or *deep*, the image's color information is and on how many colors the monitor can display. If an image file contains more color information than a monitor can display, the computer reduces the number of colors sent to the screen, so the image appears coarser than it would on a monitor that could display more colors. However, all of the color information remains stored in the file. In the reverse situation, if an image file contains less color information than the screen can display, the greater color range of the monitor cannot improve the color range of the image or make it appear less coarse (2).

1-BIT COLOR Each of the switches a computer uses to store information employs 1 bit of data to record whether the switch is OFF or ON. (*Bit* is short for *binary digit*; there are just two binary digits: 0 and 1.) A *black-and-white* image has only one switch (and therefore 1 bit) associated with each of its pixels: A pixel can be either OFF (0, unlit, black) or ON (1, lit, white) (3).

GRAYSCALE In computer parlance, 8 bits form a *byte*, the next bigger unit of information. So 8-bit color is a logical step up from 1-bit color. With 8 bits (or switches) available to describe the color of each pixel, computers can store information for a *grayscale*, a series of shades between black and white. Turning on

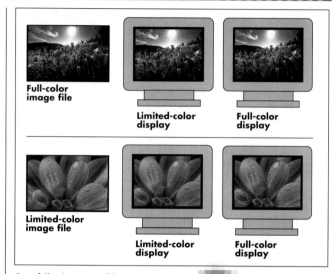

Full-color image file

Limited-color display

Full-color display

Limited-color image file

Limited-color display

Full-color display

2 A full-color image file displayed on a monitor with fewer colors looks coarser than it would on a monitor with a greater color range (top). A limited-color image is not improved by displaying it on a full-color monitor (bottom).

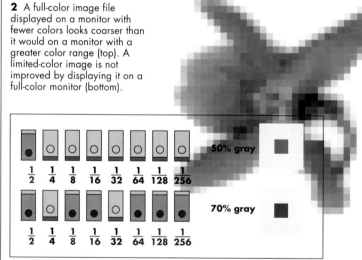

$\frac{1}{2}$ $\frac{1}{4}$ $\frac{1}{8}$ $\frac{1}{16}$ $\frac{1}{32}$ $\frac{1}{64}$ $\frac{1}{128}$ $\frac{1}{256}$

50% gray

$\frac{1}{2}$ $\frac{1}{4}$ $\frac{1}{8}$ $\frac{1}{16}$ $\frac{1}{32}$ $\frac{1}{64}$ $\frac{1}{128}$ $\frac{1}{256}$

70% gray

4 In 8-bit grayscale color representation, we can think of each of the 8 switches, or bits, as representing a different fraction of the maximum brightness that a pixel can be. For instance, one switch controls ½ the brightness, one controls another ¼ of the brightness, one controls another ⅛ of the brightness, and so on. If all the switches are turned ON, the pixel is white; if all are OFF, the pixel is black; any other combination of OFFs and ONs produces one of 254 shades of gray. A computer monitor or a graphics program that works in grayscale includes no information about hue or saturation, but it does include a relatively full range of brightness.

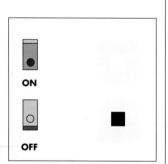

ON

OFF

3 In 1-bit color representation, the "color" data includes no hue or saturation information, and only minimal information about brightness; it tells only whether there is light or no light, whether a single switch controlling a particular pixel is ON or OFF.

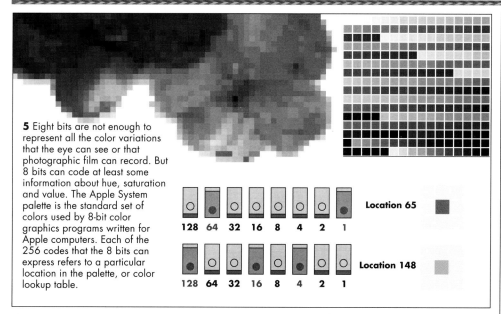

5 Eight bits are not enough to represent all the color variations that the eye can see or that photographic film can record. But 8 bits can code at least some information about hue, saturation and value. The Apple System palette is the standard set of colors used by 8-bit color graphics programs written for Apple computers. Each of the 256 codes that the 8 bits can express refers to a particular location in the palette, or color lookup table.

Location 65
128 64 32 16 8 4 2 1

Location 148
128 64 32 16 8 4 2 1

the 8 switches in various combinations gives you 256 possible levels of gray (black, white and 254 others) (4).

8-BIT COLOR A *color lookup table* provides another way to use 8 switches. In a lookup table the 256 OFF-ON combinations represent locations in RAM where color information can be found. A computer graphics program can set each of the 8 switches per pixel to represent a number and then add up the numbers represented by switches in the ON position to arrive at a code number for the color of that pixel. The code identifies one of 256 locations in the color lookup table. In its 256 locations, the table can contain a standard palette of colors that have been chosen to do a pretty good job of representing the whole range of colors in the spectrum (5).

INDEXING COLOR Instead of using a standard palette of preselected colors (such as the Apple System palette for the Macintosh desktop), some graphics programs can create an 8-bit *adaptive*, or *indexed*, palette, filling the 256 locations of the lookup table with the colors that occur most frequently in a particular image (6). With this adaptive palette, the desktop color system can produce a more realistic-looking 8-bit color version of a 24-bit color image (24-bit color is discussed on page 14).

DITHERING To make colors in addition to the 256 in a standard or indexed palette, 8-bit color systems can use *dithering* (7). Dots of two or more colors are alternated in a pattern to create the impression of another color. *Random*, or *diffusion*, *dithers* are

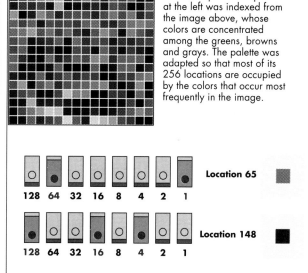

6 The adaptive 8-bit palette at the left was indexed from the image above, whose colors are concentrated among the greens, browns and grays. The palette was adapted so that most of its 256 locations are occupied by the colors that occur most frequently in the image.

Location 65
128 64 32 16 8 4 2 1

Location 148
128 64 32 16 8 4 2 1

7 This detail shows the use of dithering to represent flesh tones that are not found among the 256 colors in the picture's indexed palette. At high magnification the individual pixels and their colors are apparent, but at a lesser enlargement the dithering tricks the eye into seeing intermediate colors.

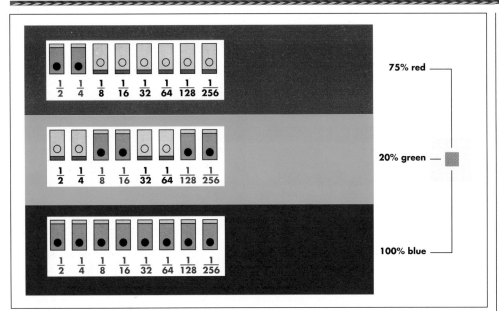

75% red

20% green

100% blue

8 In 24-bit color, each pixel is defined by 8 bits of information for each of the primaries: red, green and blue. With the potential to show over 16 million colors, 24-bit representation can provide rich, realistic color.

typically used when the goal is inconspicuous mixing; *patterned dithers* can create special graphic effects.

16-BIT COLOR With 16 bits available, thousands of colors can be displayed. Especially with custom indexing, 16 bits provide a close approximation of full color.

24-BIT COLOR In 24-bit color, each of the additive primaries (red, green and blue) is represented by an 8-bit brightness range. With 256 possibilities for each color component, theoretically 256 x 256 x 256—or 16,777,216—colors can be expressed when the three 8-bit sets of color information are combined (8). Twenty-four-bit color looks very rich and realistic (9).

32-BIT COLOR Some color graphics programs use 32 bits to describe the color of each pixel in an image. Along with the 24 bits of information about hue, saturation and value, 8 more bits describe transparency, with 256 different transparency levels from fully opaque to completely invisible (like clear glass). In a composite image, for example, these transparency levels can be

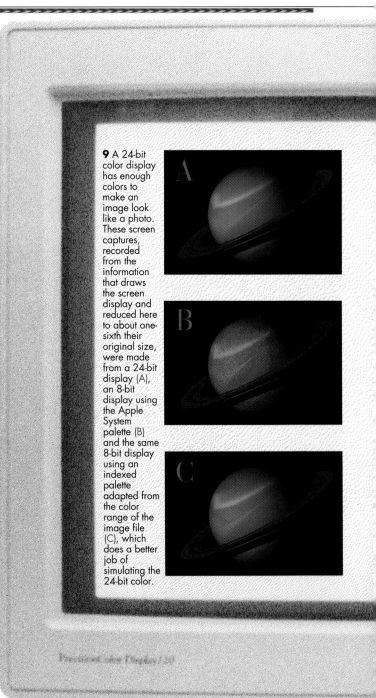

9 A 24-bit color display has enough colors to make an image look like a photo. These screen captures, recorded from the information that draws the screen display and reduced here to about one-sixth their original size, were made from a 24-bit display (A), an 8-bit display using the Apple System palette (B) and the same 8-bit display using an indexed palette adapted from the color range of the image file (C), which does a better job of simulating the 24-bit color.

In 32-bit color, starting with this

and pasting this over it

results in this.

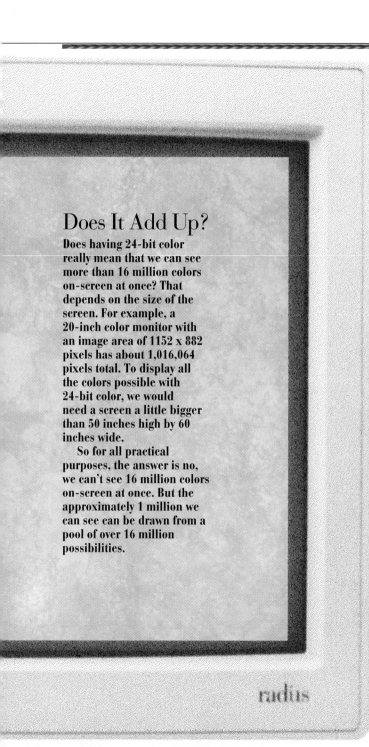

Does It Add Up?

Does having 24-bit color really mean that we can see more than 16 million colors on-screen at once? That depends on the size of the screen. For example, a 20-inch color monitor with an image area of 1152 x 882 pixels has about 1,016,064 pixels total. To display all the colors possible with 24-bit color, we would need a screen a little bigger than 50 inches high by 60 inches wide.

 So for all practical purposes, the answer is no, we can't see 16 million colors on-screen at once. But the approximately 1 million we can see can be drawn from a pool of over 16 million possibilities.

radius

used to determine how much one image allows another image "underneath" it to show through (10). When two images are combined in a color graphics program that uses 32-bit color, the program does the calculations necessary to determine what color each of the pixels in the combined image will be. It arrives at a final 24-bit image, which is then displayed to the screen or printed.

10 In the top row the nebula image was electronically pasted over the flower. In the middle row the 8 extra bits in the 32-bit color file were used to assign a transparency of 50% during the pasting operation. In the bottom row the nebula image was made 25% transparent (75% opaque).

ORIGINALLY DESKTOP COLOR GRAPHICS PROGRAMS produced two fundamentally different kinds of artwork: *bitmapped* (also called *raster-based*) and *object-oriented* (also called *vector-based*). Technically, the difference lay in the way the graphics software told the computer, display monitor or printer to form the image. Aesthetically, the difference lay in the way the artist interacted with the program (the *interface*) and in the way the artwork looked. Now the capabilities of the two kinds of software are expanding and overlapping, but to understand how graphics programs work, looking at the fundamental differences is still worthwhile.

11 Purely bitmapped artwork is a mosaic of tiny dots whose size depends on the *resolution* (number of dots per inch) at which the image is painted. Because the dots don't "know" what graphic elements they belong to, it's difficult to select one part of a picture without leaving some of it behind or taking along unrelated parts. In addition, moving part of an image leaves a "hole" with the background color showing through.

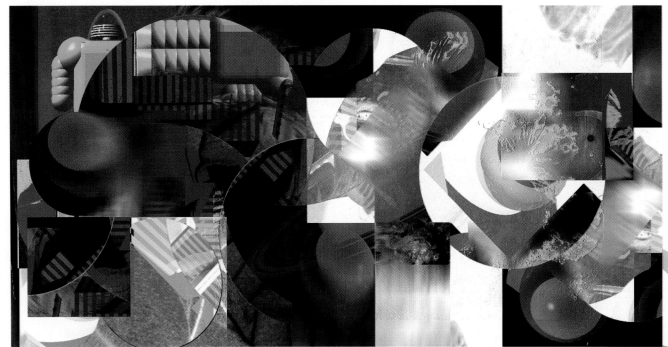

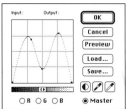

12 In image-editing programs such as Adobe Photoshop, paint tools are joined by sophisticated functions for color correction, masking and special effects. Such software can combine many kinds of files and can even convert graphic objects to bitmaps.

PIXEL-BASED COLOR PROGRAMS: "PAINTERLY" FREEDOM Pixel-based, or bitmap, programs instruct the computer to build an image that's like a mosaic, or a gridded map, of tiny square dots, or picture elements (called *pixels*). Each dot is described exactly, in terms of its size, color and position in the overall image. Viewed from a distance, the individual dots blend to form a unified picture, often one that looks like a painting or a photo. Because the picture is defined dot by dot, moving part of the picture wrecks the image, revealing bare background beneath the uprooted dots and obliterating other dots covered up by the transplant (11). The interfaces of raster-based programs tend to imitate the tools and skills used in painting and photo-retouching (called *image editing* in desktop graphics parlance) (12). (For more about painting and image-editing software, see Chapter 5.)

OBJECT-ORIENTED DRAWING PROGRAMS: PRECISION, FLEXIBILITY The instructions that an object-oriented program gives to the computer, monitor or printer are in the form of equations for objects such as lines, curves and color-filled shapes. These objects can be layered on top of one another. Like a collage of cut paper before the pieces are glued down, the objects can be moved without destroying other parts of the image. These electronic elements provide an advantage over their paper counterparts, however; we can resize, reshape or recolor the individual pieces without having to start over (13). This flexibility provides freedom to experiment in creating the original piece and also in replicating all or part of it so we can reuse it in another work. The tools and techniques provided by the interfaces of object-oriented programs are ideal for tasks that require precise construction or arrangement of parts, such as technical drawing (14). (For more about PostScript-language-based programs, see Chapter 4.)

13 Illustration programs based on Adobe Systems, Inc.'s PostScript language are the most popular object-oriented programs used for desktop graphics. In these programs a graphic element can be selected and moved as a unit, leaving other shapes untouched. Elements can have "holes" in them, as shown here, so that objects underneath show through.

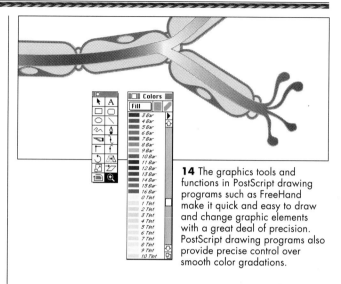

14 The graphics tools and functions in PostScript drawing programs such as FreeHand make it quick and easy to draw and change graphic elements with a great deal of precision. PostScript drawing programs also provide precise control over smooth color gradations.

Using the Term *Bitmapped*

The first computer graphics were patterns of black and white pixels. Since only two colors were involved, the color of each pixel could be described with a single bit of computer data (refer to "1-Bit Color" on page 12). Thus, the term *bitmap* came into use. The term *object-oriented* was added to the language of computer graphics to distinguish mathematically described lines and shapes from the bitmapped graphics that had to be described pixel by pixel.

In the pixel-based color graphics that followed, the term *bitmap* wasn't strictly appropriate, since the pixels could no longer be described with a single bit. *Grayscale* is commonly used to describe graphics whose pixels vary only in brightness, while *continuous-tone* began to be used to describe digitized color photos. But the term *bitmapped color*, although not exactly accurate, survives in common use, much as the term *halftone screen* is applied in the digital separation process long after the original etched screens have disappeared from everyday printing (see Chapter 6 for more about digital halftone screens).

3D PROGRAMS: A UNIQUE COMBINATION Three-dimensional graphics programs combine object-oriented modeling functions with pixel-level rendering. Modeling creates 3D objects, which can then be assigned surface characteristics, assembled into a "scene" and lighted (15). By moving the point of view, new renderings of the scene can be made without any further drawing.

15 In a 3D program, modeling produces three-dimensional objects. Once objects have been modeled and assigned surface characteristics, 3D software allows them to be lighted and "photographed" from different angles without having to redraw the objects.

Aiming for Consistent Color

Although the digital information locked in a desktop color graphics file stays constant, the way one monitor displays this information can be quite different from the way another monitor displays it or the way it looks on the printed page. That's because every device that produces color in a computer system has its own particular "fingerprint" of color characteristics. For instance, despite careful tuning, a color scanner may impart a slight red cast to the images it scans. And the color displayed on a monitor depends not only on how the monitor was adjusted before it left the factory but also on how old it is (the color system changes with age), when it was last calibrated to the manufacturer's standard and how long it has been turned on (that is, how warm it is). To further complicate the situation, different types of color printers and imagesetters produce cyan, magenta, yellow and black dots by means of different mechanical, thermal or optical systems. And even within a particular model of printer, there can be individual variations due to the color materials used, the operating conditions and the maintenance of the machinery.

For some designers working on computer systems, it's essential to be able to make judgments about what the final printed color will look like, based on the color that appears on the monitor screen. The first step in producing consistent color is to keep the hardware components performing consistently by periodically *calibrating* each one—that is, adjusting it to the manufacturer's color standard for that model.

Once the individual components have been calibrated, a *color management system* can be used to make color as consistent as possible from one calibrated device to another. Or back-to-front calibration can be done; the monitor is adjusted based on what a test of the final output looks like. Calibration and color management are described in Chapter 6.

PAGE LAYOUT PROGRAMS: ASSEMBLING THE ARTWORK

Much of the artwork that's produced in graphics programs ends up being assembled in page layout programs, which can not only accept graphics files but can also create lines and relatively simple shapes, as well as text. Colors may be imported along with artwork, or they may be specified within the page layout program (16).

16 PostScript-based page layout programs such as QuarkXPress are equipped to accept artwork in many graphics formats; to position, resize and crop the artwork; and even in some cases to assign colors to it.

Graphics File Formats

Each painting, image-editing or drawing program produces its artwork files in a format that it can reopen later for editing or printing. But because much of this artwork produced on the desktop is assembled into larger or more complex works, graphics files often need to be passed to other programs. Since not all graphics programs read one another's file formats, several standard formats have been developed, and are continually being improved upon, to make the transfer possible. Typically, page layout programs, which assemble artwork and text, can accept many file formats. Image-editing programs can accept and also produce several different formats. Here are some of the most widely compatible desktop graphics formats that can accommodate full (24-bit) color:

PS (for PostScript) A text file written in the PostScript computer language stores the instructions used to produce an object-oriented graphic. A file in PS format can produce an image on a PostScript-based printer or film recorder, but (except on the NeXT computer, for example, which has a PostScript screen display) it can't produce an image on-screen. However, the PS format is compact and can easily be opened and resaved in EPS format (see below) when an on-screen image is needed.

EPS or EPSF (for encapsulated PostScript format) A PostScript text file is combined with a PICT or PICT2 component (see below) so the image can be displayed on-screen and printed from non-PostScript-based as well as PostScript-based output devices. EPS files are accepted by virtually all page layout programs that run on the most widely used desktop computers, Macintoshes and IBM PCs (and similar systems, called *clones*). DCS is a specialized EPS format that stores an image in the four component plates that will print the process ink colors—C, M, Y and K—with one PS file for each of the four separations. In addition, the file includes a PICT2 component for screen display. One advantage of the DCS format is that bitmapped images can be color-separated for printing individually (different line screens can be "locked in" to each image) rather than all the images in a publication being subjected to identical treatment through a page layout program.

PICT and PICT2 These formats store object-oriented drawings in a form that can be interpreted by Macintosh computers for display on-screen or output on non-PostScript printers. They can also incorporate bitmapped image information. PICT formats are used when an image is to be displayed on-screen, but they generally don't work well for color separations and printing.

TIFF (for tagged-image file format) TIFF is the most universally accepted format for storing bitmap information on desktop systems. Many scanners save images in this format. TIFF formats include 1-bit (black-and-white), grayscale, RGB and CMYK.

Scitex CT (for continuous-tone) Some desktop graphics programs can accept and produce bitmap information in this format so it can be passed to or from the high-end Scitex imaging system.

PCX Used on IBM PCs and clones, PCX is similar to TIFF, though not as widely accepted.

TGA (for Targa) This bitmap format, particularly good for video or slide output, is not widely supported in page layout programs.

PART OF THE INTERFACE of every color graphics program is some kind of color picker, a tool that allows us to choose colors for painting or drawing. Among the various interfaces, colors can be selected from a program palette (17), a custom palette, mixed by eye (especially in bitmapped programs) (18), or specified by composition (19). Most color graphics programs provide more than one of these three options.

ASSEMBLING A PALETTE Since color is so important in the way people respond to design and illustration, choosing colors is one of the most important tasks in determining a project's success. Desktop graphics programs can help in several ways:

• Colors can be chosen according to their relative positions on the color wheel, as described on page 6. Some color graphics programs have built-in devices to help with the process—for example, by providing an on-screen color wheel (20) or by allowing the artist to choose related colors somewhat automatically (21).

• Another way to select a palette of harmonious colors is to use an image-editing program to help you take a cue from nature (22).

• Sometimes it's important to match an existing palette—for example, to produce an illustration that's part of a series. In some programs you can open a file and delete the image itself but retain the palette. In other cases the old and new images can be opened at the same time and colors can be sampled from the old one and reused in the new.

Two important considerations in assembling colors for a palette are avoiding trapping problems (see page 42) and minimizing the occurrence of *moiré*, an unintended pattern that can develop in printing with halftone screens (see page 62).

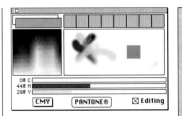

18 ColorStudio, like many other painting and image-editing programs, provides an area where colors can be mixed and then selected for use with the painting tools.

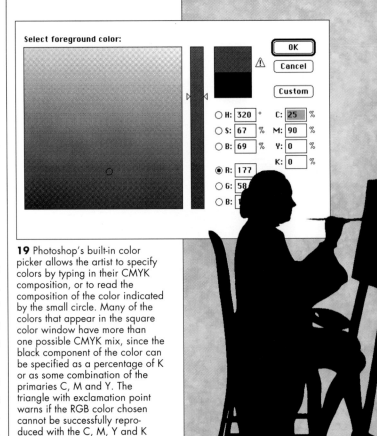

19 Photoshop's built-in color picker allows the artist to specify colors by typing in their CMYK composition, or to read the composition of the color indicated by the small circle. Many of the colors that appear in the square color window have more than one possible CMYK mix, since the black component of the color can be specified as a percentage of K or as some combination of the primaries C, M and Y. The triangle with exclamation point warns if the RGB color chosen cannot be successfully reproduced with the C, M, Y and K process printing inks.

17 In addition to colors that the artist can specify, PageMaker's basic palette supplies Paper and Registration colors, especially useful in page layout programs, where artwork and text blocks are assembled. Paper can be used to fill objects that will be used to mask items that shouldn't print. Assigning the Registration color to an object causes it to print on all plates when the file is color-separated.

Color Matching Systems

In the past, process color, with its overprinted halftone dot patterns of cyan, magenta, yellow and black inks (CMYK), was used mostly for reproducing color photographs or for printing documents that contained lots of them. Most other color printing was done with custom-mixed ink colors such as those of the Pantone Matching System (see page 5). As desktop publishing technology has made it easier and less expensive to produce the film separations needed for process color, more color printing is being done by this method.

The desktop artist, working with the colors displayed on-screen, also needs to know how these colors are likely to look on paper. Color swatching systems offer printed color samples, along with formulas for producing them from tints of process inks. Being able to choose target colors from a printed color swatching system and then to specify those colors in the graphics program improves our chances of getting predictable printed colors.

The Pantone Process Color System is one of several swatching systems that can be used to specify process colors for predictable printed results. A fan-deck guide shows more than 3000 process tints, organized chromatically and printed with commercially available screen values.

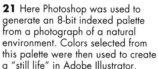

20 The Apple color picker, available through Macintosh color graphics programs, reproduces the color wheel so complements, triads and so forth can be chosen by their relative positions on the wheel.

22 PixelPaint Professional, a color painting program, provides several preselected palettes of colors, including this "Peaceful" combination, for artists to use "as is" or as starting points for assembling their own palettes. The program also has a Color Theory color picker that can generate a basic palette of nearby hues, complements, shades and tints for any color the artist chooses.

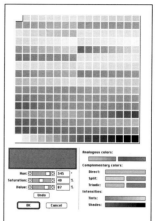

21 Here Photoshop was used to generate an 8-bit indexed palette from a photograph of a natural environment. Colors selected from this palette were then used to create a "still life" in Adobe Illustrator.

3

Input and Storage Options

Input to Desktop Color Systems
Resolution
Storage and File Compression

WITH TRADITIONAL GRAPHIC DESIGN tools and techniques, once the artist begins developing an idea, the next step is to commit the concept to paper with ink, pencil or markers. In digital design, the comparable first step is input—recording the concept in the computer's memory.

MICE, TABLETS AND OTHER DRAWING TOOLS

The mouse was the first widely used desktop input device for designers and illustrators. Although many digital artists are very comfortable drawing and painting with a mouse, some complain that it's like trying to draw with a bar of soap. Mini-mice and trackballs add finer and more direct control, but the best solution for desktop drawing and painting seems to be the graphics tablet with stylus. Besides providing the free motion characteristic of a brush or pen, a stylus and tablet can be programmed to respond to pressure. This gives a more natural "feel" to digital artwork with both raster-based (1) and object-oriented (2) drawing programs.

IMPORTING IMAGES For reproduction of photos and for raster-based artwork that starts with photographic material, another sort of input predominates: Images can be scanned from film or prints or "grabbed" from live video or videotape (see "Video Input" on page 27).

Successful digital reproduction of photos depends more on the quality of the original image than on anything you do to it later with image-editing software. To select a high-quality original, use these criteria:
• The image should be sharp and in focus.
• You should be able to see detail in the highlight, midtone and shadow areas (3).
• Contrast should be good, with bright whites, deep blacks and a large number of brightness levels in between (4).
• Color should be balanced, without a color cast that makes the image look green or red, for example.

1 A graphics tablet with pressure-sensitive stylus can be used to produce some very "painterly" effects, as shown in these flowers created with Fractal Design Painter.

 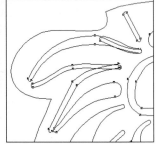

2 When a pressure-sensitive tablet is used with a PostScript illustration program, the result can be a line that looks hand-drawn. This image was created in FreeHand. The colored flowers and leaves were drawn with the curve tool and were given linear or radial fills. The black "strokes" were created with the pressure-sensitive freehand tool. The program automatically captured the strokes as filled shapes.

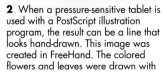

The quality you need in the original image depends, of course, on what you intend to do with it. If you plan to fill an 8 x 10-inch page with a fashion photo, you'll need high-quality input. But if you plan to use the image as source material for a montage created with special effects and applied patterns and textures, high quality in the original may not be paramount (5).

SCANNING Once you select an appropriate original, the next step is to scan it. The quality of the scanned image depends on the scanning system's ability to pick up the full range of color information from the film or print; to make the scan at the appropriate resolution (see "Resolution" on page 28); to quickly and accurately sharpen the image, correct color and adjust brightness and contrast; and to crop and straighten the image as the scan is being made. Some scanning systems even convert RGB color information into the CMYK system, arriving at an image that's ready for desktop color separation. The better a scanning system can do these things, the less correcting and retouching will have to be done later with image-editing software. And to the degree that these scan-related tasks are automated, you can save time in the scanning process. If the scan is made on your desktop, any manual adjustments you have to make will cost you time. If the scan is

3 When choosing an original photograph for desktop reproduction, look for detail in the highlights, midtones and shadows. Of the two versions of the photo shown here, the right image shows more midtone detail.

Scanning 3-D Objects

Desktop scanners are not limited to scanning photographs. In fact, any solid object small enough to fit in the scanner's image area can be captured on disk. For a white background, close the lid on thin objects or use a piece of white foam-core board supported by shims behind a thicker object. Place objects upside down if necessary, to get the shadow where you want it. The resulting images are not the sort of quality that could be used for product shots or magazine covers, but such scans are more than adequate for comprehensive sketches, and they can even be the basis for some interesting final illustrations.

The crayon and flower illustrations shown here began with some of the objects at top right scanned on a desktop flatbed scanner. The crayons were treated with Adobe Photoshop's Find Edges filter. The flowers were given a three-level posterization, also in Photoshop, and then the Poster Edges filter from Aldus Gallery Effects was applied to produce the black edges.

4 Good contrast is important in choosing a photo to be scanned. In general, photos should have definite and distinct black and white elements, but also a broad range of tones in between (top). Too much contrast in the original (middle) or too little (bottom) results in a reproduction with too little detail or not enough "snap."

made at a service bureau, these changes take the service technician's time and consequently cost you money.

HOW SCANNERS WORK A scanner copies an image by taking a series of samples. Light is beamed at thousands of tiny points on the original and transmitted (in the case of a film original) or reflected (from a paper print). The color of the transmitted or reflected light is picked up by the scanner's sensing apparatus and recorded as digital information (6). Two different technologies are used for sensing the light: charge-coupled devices (CCDs) and photomultiplier tubes (PMTs). Each of the technologies has advantages and disadvantages.

Scanners that use CCDs typically move the scan head (a row of devices for sensing the red, green and blue components of light) past the photo or object to be scanned. The CCDs detect the amount of red, green and blue being reflected from or transmitted through each scan point. This light information is translated into electrical energy and then converted from analog form (the amount of energy present) to digital form (discrete numbers that can be stored as a digital graphics file). The stored information is a set of numbers (often saved as a TIFF file), a collection of the color data for all the sample points in the image.

Scanners with PMT technology typically have a drum that moves the art, while the scan head stays still. PMTs tend to be more sensitive at low light levels than CCDs, so they pick up color better in dark areas of the photo.

PMT technology is more expensive than CCD. Other scanner characteristics that affect both quality and cost include the mechanism that moves either the original or the scan head. In general, drum scanners offer better control of the light beam than scanners that move the scan head past the document. Precision of motion increases sharpness, as does the quality of the lenses and mirrors used to focus the reflected light.

5 If the image you start with will be modified with montage and special effects, the quality of the original photo may not be too important.

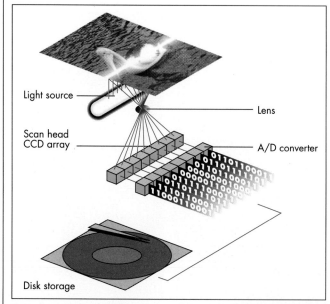

6 A scanner uses a light source similar to the bulb in a slide projector to bounce light off or transmit light through the original image. An optical system directs the light from the original to a scan head that senses its red, green and blue components. The light signals are converted to electrical signals, which are then converted to digital information and recorded in a graphics file.

The resolution (that is, the number of samples per inch) that a scanner can achieve can also be important to image quality. Most standard desktop scanners provide a top resolution of 300, 400 or 600 samples per inch. For transparency scanners, resolution is often expressed in terms of "K," for *kilo*, or *thousand*. A 2K scanner, for example, takes 2000 readings over the long dimension of an original, regardless of how big the original is. That's how a 35mm slide scanner can get enough information to allow the scanned image to be enlarged successfully.

Because scanners record light, the information they pick up is RGB color data. Many scanners store the information in this form, but some convert the RGB data to CMYK separations. The high-end scanning systems used before desktop color separation was available (for example, the Scitex system) use PMT technology and also have extremely good RGB-to-CMYK conversion algorithms. Such scans have decreased in cost, so desktop designers sometimes start with high-end scans.

The scanning system you choose will depend on the results you need, the time you can afford to spend adjusting the scan and the expertise you bring to the project. The highest-quality, easiest-to-use scans provide (a) a dynamic range that will record the full range of color density in the original; (b) the ability to focus sharply; (c) the ability to maintain calibration (or recalibrate easily) so it's possible to get predictable, repeatable results; and (d) software that automates or simplifies trial scans, color and contrast adjustment, sharpening, straightening, cropping and, if the scan will eventually be used in print, color conversion to CMYK.

SCANNED IMAGES ON CD-ROM CD-ROM is an ideal medium for supplying photographic images to the desktop because a single disc can hold over 500 MB of data. Several stock photo companies supply their images on CD-ROM. Of course, the quality varies, depending on the quality of the original photo and of the scanning.

VIDEO INPUT Another source of images for use on the desktop is video. Images from live video, videocassette, videodiscs or still-video cameras can be brought into desktop computers through a video *frame grabber*, a circuit board that translates the image into a format the computer can accept. Frame grabbers that capture the red, green and blue signals separately and then merge them into a 24-bit color file, rather than grabbing the composite signal, give higher-quality images.

Video grabs are low-resolution images. To be used in printed materials, they have to be resampled to a higher resolution and then sharpened, again to improve image quality. The final result is never as good as film quality, but video images can be very useful—they can be used immediately, sometimes they are the only existing pictures of an event, and they can provide interesting material for image manipulation.

Photo CD

The Kodak Photo CD system delivers relatively high-quality scanned images from 35mm slides or negatives on a CD-ROM disk. Two products in the Photo CD line—Photo CD Master and Pro Photo CD Master—can be particularly useful as input for desktop publishing. (A third product, Print Photo CD, can be used for output and storage.)

A Photo CD or Pro Photo CD disk can be ordered when new film is originally processed, to be delivered along with the slides or prints from the film. You can also have as many as 100 previously developed slides or negatives put onto a Photo CD disk. The images can be loaded into any desktop computer equipped with a compatible CD-ROM drive and Photo CD acquisition software, which can be bought as a stand-alone program or supplied along with popular image-editing or page layout software. Once acquired, the pictures can be used like any other scanned images. (For up-to-date information about Photo CD–compatible CD-ROM drives and software, contact Kodak's Digital and Applied Imaging Support Center at 800-235-6325. For a more general introduction to Photo CD products, see *The Photo CD Book*, from Verbum Books.)

Besides the quality of the scans and their low price, another advantage of Photo CD images is that they are available in five different resolutions (or six, with Pro Photo CD). The highest Photo CD Master resolution (shown below) allows for a high degree of enlargement without the appearance of obvious pixels. The lower-resolution files are efficiently sized to be used for thumbnail sketches, for position only in graphic design, for on-screen presentations and multimedia and for printing at small sizes.

Pro Photo CD's sixth resolution allows even greater enlargement than Photo CD Master. It can also accommodate originals larger than 35 mm—up to 4 x 5 inches.

RESOLUTION IS A MEASURE of how detailed an image is—that is, how much information is recorded, stored, displayed or output over a particular linear distance. In electronic design the term is used to cover several related but quite distinct kinds of measurement.

SCAN RESOLUTION Scan resolution can be expressed as *samples per inch* (7).

The higher the resolution, the more information is recorded in the scan. The more information, the more enlargement the image can take. But the bigger the file, the more space is needed to store it and the more time is needed to refresh the screen as you work on it.

DISPLAY RESOLUTION Display resolution is a function of the monitor on which a graphics file is displayed—often 72 or 75 *pixels per inch* (ppi). An image scanned at 300 samples per inch would appear at four times its actual size on-screen at 75 pixels per inch (8). When you work on an image that will eventually be printed, viewing it at a 1:1 enlargement—that is, showing 1 pixel on-screen for each pixel in the file—gives the most accurate view of color in the file. Even though the 1:1 enlargement displays the image at two to four times its eventual printed size, this enlargement is the most useful for evaluating color.

OUTPUT RESOLUTION Output resolution is usually expressed as the number of *dots per linear inch* (dpi) the output device puts on the film or paper. Output resolution is device-dependent—that is, it's limited by the capabilities of the output device. Desktop printers can typically print 300, 400 or 600 dpi on paper, while imagesetters can produce 600, 1200 or 2400 dpi or other high resolutions on paper or film.

7 Since scan resolution (in samples per inch) is a linear measurement, doubling the resolution of a scan means that four times as much information can be recorded from the same area of the original image. A single scan point records one pixel of information, but doubling the resolution records four times as many pixels, and thus four times as much information, for the same point on the image.

Continuous-tone print scanned at 300 samples per inch

5 inches
4 inches
1500 samples
1200 samples

20.8 inches
16.7 inches

On-screen image displayed at 72 dpi

1500 pixels
1200 pixels

Image displayed on Apple high-resolution 13-inch RGB monitor

5 inches
4 inches
750 lines
600 lines

Final image printed at 150 lines per inch

---

8 The display resolution built into most monitors requires that an image scanned at 300 dpi be enlarged about four times to be shown accurately on-screen. Although the image seems suddenly much larger than it was, this temporary enlargement for display doesn't change the size of the recorded image.

9 Halftone screen resolution determines how many rows of halftone cells there can be in a linear inch. The dots within the cells can vary in size. Small dots of a particular process color are found in areas where that color contributes little to the color of the image. Large dots, completely filling the cell, mean solid coverage of that particular color.

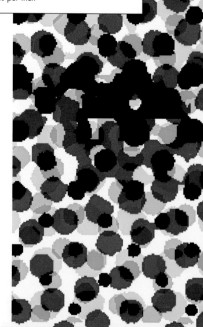

HALFTONE SCREEN RESOLUTION Halftone screen resolution, or *screen ruling*, refers to the density of halftone *cells* in the fine screens traditionally used for printing. The cell is the maximum space that can be filled by a halftone dot. The dot can completely fill the cell, or it can be much smaller (9). In digital halftone screens, each halftone dot is made up of even tinier output dots, and the number of output dots per halftone cell is important in determining the quality of the final printed piece. (For more about the relationship between output resolution and screen resolution, see Chapter 6.) Screen resolution is expressed in *lines per inch* (lpi).

RESOLUTION RATIOS A rule of thumb for getting the best quality when you print a scanned image is that there should be a 2:1 ratio of scan resolution (samples per inch) to halftone screen resolution (lines per inch) (10), although for some images this ratio can be as low as 1.25:1 without degrading the image.

It isn't too difficult to understand how the 2:1 rule of thumb is arrived at. It's clear that there has to be at least 1 sample per inch (scan resolution) for each line per inch (halftone screen resolution). That way, there is at least 1 scan dot of information to tell the output device how big to make the process color dot for each halftone cell. Less than a 1:1 ratio would definitely produce an image of lower quality. That's because the imagesetter, failing to find a scan dot's worth of information for each halftone dot it needs to construct, has to interpolate (that is, make an educated guess) to fill in the missing information, thus degrading the image (11).

Up to a point, the quality of the printed image can be improved by increasing the ratio of scan resolution to screen resolution above 1:1. For instance, for a publication printed at 150 lines per inch, images could be scanned at 300 dpi to get a 2:1 ratio of scan resolution to screen resolution. At a scan-to-screen resolution of more than 2:1, however, the extra information seems to be wasted. It doesn't improve the printed image, but it does increase the file size, which slows down the operation of an image-editing program and increases the amount of storage space needed.

If an image will be printed larger than the original from which it was scanned, however, the scan resolution will have to be higher in order to get the same 2:1 ratio. For instance, if an image is to be enlarged 200 percent, a scan resolution of 600 samples per inch must be used to get a 2:1 ratio for output at 150 lpi.

10 The extra information gained by using a scan resolution twice the halftone screen resolution allows the software that creates the halftone screen to double-check the composition of the halftone dots, leading to a better printed image. This extra resolution can be especially helpful for smooth rendition of straight lines that appear at angles other than vertical or horizontal.

11 The image on the left was scanned at 50 samples per inch, the one on the right at 200 samples per inch. Both were printed at the 150 lpi halftone screen resolution used to make the color separations for this book. Notice that the lower scan resolution produces a poorer image, because some of the data used to form the halftone dots had to be "invented." Although the software that does the inventing uses color and brightness information in the image itself to arrive at the best guesses to fill in the missing information, it can never do as good a job as if enough data had been available in the image file.

SCAN FILES AND OTHER COLOR IMAGES can be huge. An 8 x 10-inch full-color (24-bit) image scanned at 300 samples per inch and saved in the RGB color system amounts to over 21 megabytes (MB) of information. So designers who work with color bitmaps need lots of storage space, both active (for work in progress) and archival (for images that may be needed again in the future).

ACTIVE STORAGE Active storage, the kind that lets you load and save images from within graphics software, needs to be able to hold several files, make them available reasonably quickly, and, in some cases, be portable. It's easy to tell how a floppy disk, hard disk, removable hard disk or other medium stacks up with regard to the first criterion—just look at the "megabytage."

The 20, 40 and even 80 MB hard drives that were once the standards of desktop storage now seem puny to the point of frustration to artists who work with color bitmaps. Hard disk drives with 120 MB, 600 MB, a gigabyte (1000 MB) or more of storage space are now not uncommon in desktop studios.

The ability to pack away huge files doesn't solve the storage problem completely, however. Once the files are stored, how quickly can they be found and loaded into RAM so you can work on them? *Access time* (the time needed to find the information) and *transfer time* (the time needed to read the data from storage to RAM) become important for the large hard disk drives.

For portability, removable 44 and 88 MB SyQuest cartridges are commonly used for passing large files from designer to client and from desktop studio to imagesetting service bureau. However, optical read-write drives may become a standard for portable storage; they can store 128 MB to more than a gigabyte on a disk that's between the size of a thick floppy and that of a SyQuest cartridge. CD-ROM discs also offer a stable, convenient way to store images. Several removable SyQuest cartridges full of images can be transferred to a single CD-ROM disc.

ARCHIVAL STORAGE *Digital audiotape (DAT)* drives offer relatively safe, cheap, compact storage for desktop computer files. Five gigabytes of data can be *backed up* (copied and stored for retrieval later) on a single tape cassette. However, DAT doesn't serve as working storage because it isn't set up to pass data back and forth from tape to RAM. To retrieve an image stored on DAT, it's first copied to a working storage medium. CD-ROM storage, although not yet as inexpensive as DAT, is even more stable, and the stored data are easier to retrieve.

FILE COMPRESSION Even with the technology available for storing large files, desktop designers feel the need to compress these files in order to reduce the amount of storage space they occupy. Compression can be important in making files small enough to transport easily to service bureaus.

Another reason to compress large files is to transmit them by modem over telephone lines. To send a 21 MB image with a modem operating at 14.4 kilobaud (thousands of bits per second) would tie up the phone for hours.

Two kinds of compression—*lossless* and *lossy*—are used to temporarily reduce file size for storage, transport or transmission. After the compression algorithms have been applied to a file, the file can't be read by graphics programs until decompression algorithms restore it to its original size and structure.

Lossless compression works by a sort of "summing up" process, in which information is packaged more economically but no data are lost. It can work like this: Instead of recording a separate bit of data for each pixel in a black-and-white image—"this one is black, this one is white, this one is white, this one is white, this one is white" and so on—wherever possible, this information is encoded in fewer pieces of data—"this one is black, the next four are white" and so on.

Lossless compression doesn't "throw away" any information, so when the compressed files are decompressed, all the data can be retrieved and the image file will be the same as it was originally. But lossless compression wasn't designed for color images. You can see that this kind of compression would work better for black-and-white images than for color, where there could be over 16 million different pixel descriptions instead of just two.

Lossy compression compacts image files a great deal more than lossless compression does—to a twentieth, a fiftieth, even a hundredth of their original size. It does this by judiciously deciding what data can be thrown away, not to be retrieved when the file is decompressed. And yet at 20:1 compression, an image printed from the compressed and decompressed file often can't be distinguished from the original.

How can we throw away over 95 percent of the data in a color image and not notice the difference? Lossy compression uses the fact that the human eye is much more sensitive to luminance (the brightness information in a color image) than it is to chrominance (the hue information). Brightness and chrominance data are separated, and then lossy compression algorithms are applied to the chrominance data. Finally, a lossless compression algorithm is applied to the data to pack it even more. The result of all the compression is that later, when the files are decompressed, not all the color information can be retrieved (12).

For lossy compression, an international standard has been developed by the Joint Photographic Experts Group (JPEG). So any JPEG-based compression/decompression program should be able to decompress an image compressed with any other JPEG-based software. Different compression programs apply the JPEG algorithms differently, however, leading to differences in image quality in the compressed and then decompressed files.

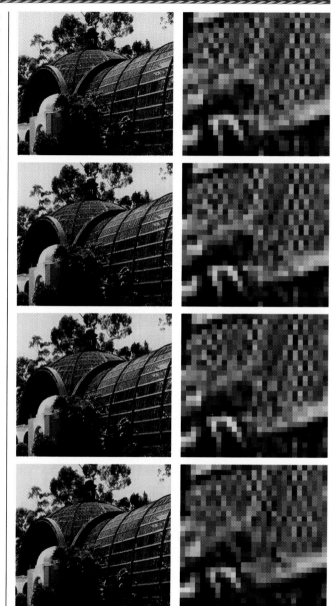

12 This image is shown without compression (top) and compressed with JPEG software at ratios of 20:1(upper middle), 50:1 (lower middle) and 100:1 (bottom). The image details are shown here after decompression. You can see that quite a bit of data can be "repackaged" or even removed through compression without deterioration of the image.

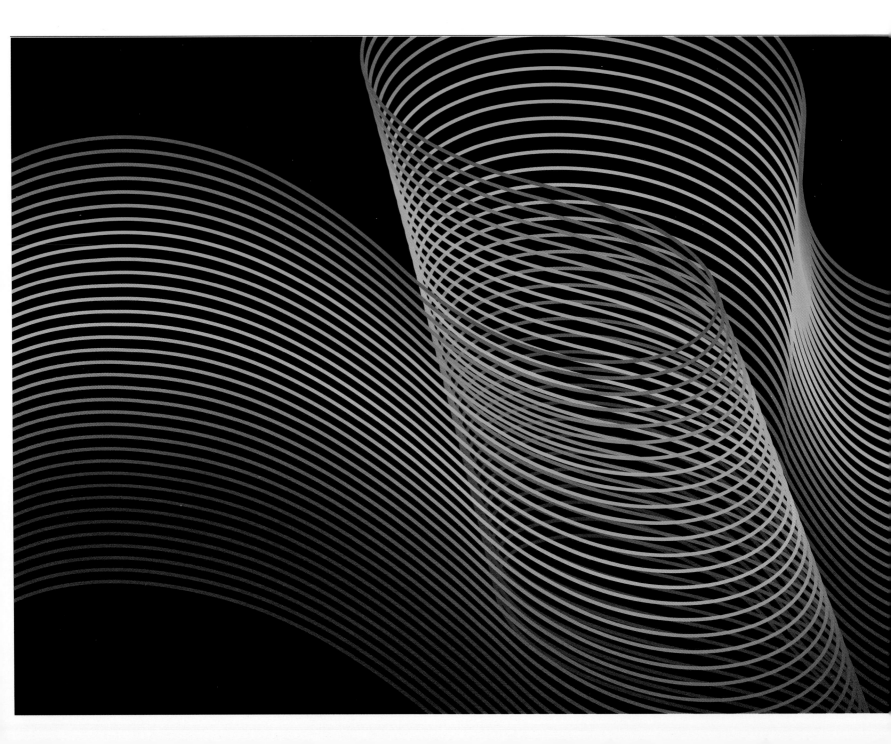

4

PostScript
Illustration

The Power of PostScript
Blends and Color Gradations
PostScript Illustration Tips
Trapping

POSTSCRIPT ILLUSTRATION PROGRAMS can't be beat for precision drawing. Regardless of which microcomputer they run on, all the widely used PostScript illustration programs share many of the same drawing, transforming and type-handling capabilities.

DRAWING PostScript drawing programs typically provide five kinds of drawing tools:

- A tool for drawing plain or patterned straight lines in any weight or color (1)
- Ellipse and rectangle tools for drawing geometric shapes (2)
- Tools for placing control points, one by one, to define a path—either an open-ended line or a closed shape (3)
- A tool that automatically places control points along a curve that the artist draws "freehand" (4)
- An autotrace tool that automatically draws a PostScript outline of an imported bitmapped image (5)

PostScript illustration software can precisely position, duplicate, link together and transform lines and shapes. Locations of objects can also be pinpointed numerically. Visible or invisible grids can help align objects by snapping them to grid points that line them up with one another or with an underlying structure established for the illustration.

PostScript drawing programs provide a flexible working environment. A *keyline view* shows only the paths that define a drawing; a *preview mode* shows the strokes, fills and colors. *Magnified views* make it possible to work on fine details. *Grouping* some elements of a drawing lets the artist select them all at once and move or otherwise transform them without accidentally knocking things out of line. *Hiding* parts of the drawing gets them out of the way and makes it easier to select and work on other parts. *Locking* leaves objects in view but guards against accidental movement or change.

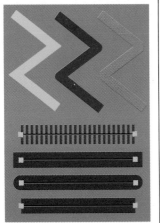

1 Every PostScript line, straight or curved, consists of a *path* and a *stroke*. The path specifies length and direction. Stroke characteristics include weight (or width), color, pattern and treatment of ends and joins. In most PostScript illustration programs half the width of the stroke extends to each side of the path. If a line has an end cap that extends beyond the path, its size also depends on the stroke width. Lines can be constrained to 45- and 90-degree or other angles.

2 Ellipse and rectangle tools define closed paths with identifiable centers. Like other closed paths, the shapes drawn with these tools can be stroked and also filled with color or with predefined PostScript patterns. These kimonos were drawn with FreeHand's shape tools.

3 Control points anchor the Bezier curves that define shapes in PostScript-based drawing programs. Handles associated with the points determine the direction and degree of curvature of the paths. Manipulating the handles can change the shape of a path, even without moving the control points.

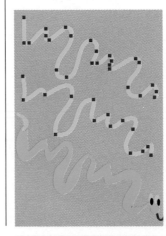

4 Freehand drawing tools can follow each small deviation in the line you draw, placing many control points (top). Or they can draw a smoother curve by placing fewer points (middle). The freehand tool can also respond to pressure, drawing a closed path that looks like the thick-and-thin stroke of a line drawn by hand (bottom). Unlike a line, however, this closed path can be given both a stroke and a fill.

5 Adobe Streamline is a PostScript-based program developed specifically for automatic tracing. More versatile than the autotrace tool in other widely used PostScript programs, the one in Adobe Streamline can trace scanned images (top) to produce stroked outlines (middle) or filled black-and-white shapes.

6 A single shape can be used to mask one or more objects. This man's jacket was rendered in Adobe Illustrator by drawing a solid-colored background shape and designating it as a mask, layering several different shapes over it, and grouping them with the larger shape.

TRANSFORMING With PostScript illustration, one shape, or *clipping path*, can trim away or mask parts of other shapes (6). And from a designer's point of view, one of the best things about computer-based artwork, and particularly about PostScript drawings, is that you don't have to send out for photostats or start over from scratch each time you need a larger, smaller or slightly reshaped version of your artwork. Objects can be scaled, rotated, skewed and reflected (7). Step-and-repeat functions can make consistent changes in size or spacing (8).

HANDLING TYPE PostScript illustration programs provide all the standard typesetting functions, letting the designer control size, leading, word spacing, letterspacing and kerning. Like other objects, type can be scaled, rotated, skewed and reflected. It can also be aligned to a path (9). Type can be converted to paths and treated like drawn objects—stroked, filled and otherwise altered, or used as a mask (10).

7 PostScript-based drawings can be instantaneously copied, scaled, rotated, skewed or reflected.

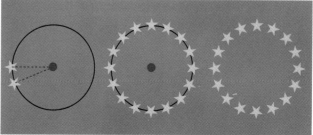

8 To make a ring of 16 stars in FreeHand, a single star was placed on a circle and then copied and rotated 24 degrees (left), with the center of the circle serving as the center of rotation. The copy-and-rotate sequence was repeated 14 more times (middle) and the circle was deleted (right).

Using Filters

Filters are subroutines, or "miniprograms," that the main program calls upon to perform special tasks. Filters increase the number of drawing functions or graphics special effects a program can perform automatically. Selecting objects and then making a single choice from a menu can bring about complex transformations, such as Adobe Illustrator's Tweak effect shown here.

Filter technology makes it easy for software developers to add power to a program without rewriting the computer code for the main body of the program. Other software developers (often called third parties) can also design filters to work with the main program.

Filters exist for both PostScript drawing programs and pixel-based graphics software. (See Chapter 5 for more about filters used with pixel-based color images.)

9 Type was fitted around the center top of one circle and the center bottom of another. The two circles were moved together until their centers overlapped exactly.

10 These letters were typeset, converted to outlines and modified to add the "teeth" at the bottoms of the letters and to reshape the opening of the "O." In compound objects such as converted type, internal shapes like the center of the "O" become "holes," allowing background to show through.

A POWERFUL AND FASCINATING FEATURE of PostScript illustration programs is their ability to automatically build a series of intermediate steps in a transition, or blend, from one object to another of a different shape, color or position (11). Most programs can also automatically fill shapes with smooth *gradations*, or fountains (12). Used in combination, blends and graduated fills can imitate the modeling effects achieved with an airbrush (13).

GOOD-LOOKING, EFFICIENT BLENDS The computer builds a color gradation as a series of small steps, or shades, between two colors. With *too few* shades, the individual steps become apparent, and a color change can look banded instead of smooth (14). But with *too many* steps in the blend it can take a long time to redraw the screen or to output a file, without any improvement in the smoothness of the gradation. How can we predict whether a particular blend has enough steps to produce a smooth color transition? And how do we know how many steps are too many?

Like many aspects of PostScript programs, the answer is rooted in arithmetic. Because of the nature of PostScript, the most shades you can have in a PostScript gradation from a 0% tint to a 100% tint of a color is 256, regardless of how big a space the color change will fill. When the change in tint is less than 100%, the number of shades available is reduced:

Maximum shades available = 256 × % change in tint

In digital halftone screening, the number of available shades also depends on the relationship between the output resolution (dots per inch) and the halftone screen density (lines per inch). Here's another way of looking at it:

$$\text{\# of shades} = \frac{\text{Maximum shades available} \times (\text{dpi/lpi})^2}{256}$$

11 This illustration for a Christmas card was created in FreeHand as a 10-step blend between the dove shape and the star. Each control point on the dove was matched by one of the 11 points on the star.

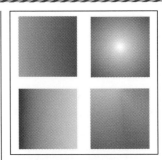

12 The PostScript drawing programs that create automatic color fountain effects usually provide them in several styles. *Graduated* fills may be *linear* (top left) or *logarithmic* (bottom left) and may be specified at any angle. In *radial* fills (top right) the color transition occurs from the center outward. Custom gradations can be created with blends of overlapping steps (bottom right).

13 Aldus FreeHand's linear, logarithmic and radial fills, which can be applied at different angles, serve well to render simple shapes and smooth surfaces, as seen in most of the modeled shapes here. But when an illustration requires irregular shapes with more complex modeling, the blend function proves more useful. The nostril on the right has a radial fill, and the neck is made from two logarithmic fills that meet in the middle; other shapes are modeled with linear fills. Both right and left cheeks are blends from a light shape to a different darker shape.

14 Visible banding of colors can spoil the look of an illustration where smooth color gradation was intended.

Notice that the calculations for the number of steps didn't address the distance over which the blend stretched. But distance definitely makes a difference with regard to banding. For instance, if your gradation can have 50 shades, the steps will probably be invisible if the transition occurs in the space of half an inch. But if it occurs over 5 inches, that makes 10 steps per inch, and banding will probably show, although improvements in the PostScript language and in output devices have cut down on the amount of banding we see. For instance, a newer screening method called *stochastic screening* helps to prevent banding. PostScript illustrations can also be output on high-end color-separation systems such as those of Scitex and Linotype-Hell, which eliminate banding by replacing PostScript gradations with their own smooth gradients. (Output resolution, halftone screen density and stochastic screening are discussed further in Chapter 6.)

For smooth blends, perform calculations with the equations on page 36. If you arrive at a number that looks too low to prevent banding, stop and rethink the blend. Can you use a higher percentage color difference, use the gradation over a smaller distance, change the output resolution or the halftone screen, or use a different output method?

MULTICOLOR BLENDS PostScript drawing programs blend between two hues defined as the starting and ending colors. But multistep blends can be constructed by putting two or more blends together. The artwork that spans pages 32 and 33 resulted from a multistep blend (15).

15 The illustration that opens this chapter started as a single curve; it was copied, and the clone was repositioned and its shape was changed a bit (left). One curve was assigned a blue color and one violet, and a four-step blend was specified (middle). The intermediate lines were assigned the other colors of the rainbow (right). Then adjacent lines were used in pairs to make five six-step blends to produce the figure on pages 32 and 33.

Color Quirks

As if the differences between RGB and CMYK color systems and the varying color characteristics of scanners, monitors and printers weren't enough for desktop artists to contend with, color confusion can also arise from the way different graphics programs represent colors on-screen. For example, to save processing time, some PostScript illustration programs show a relatively low-quality color image on-screen. Blends may look rough and banded, for instance. Through Preferences settings these programs may let you choose a higher-quality viewing option in which the process of redrawing the screen takes longer but the illustrations look more like their printed versions.

Another source of color confusion, especially with PostScript illustrations, is that a page layout program may use a different on-screen representation of color than that used by the PostScript drawing software in which an illustration was created. As a result, artwork saved in encapsulated PostScript (EPS) format and placed in a page layout may look different than it did when you were drawing it. Or a CMYK color defined in a page layout program may look different on-screen than a color with exactly the same CMYK specifications in imported artwork. But although the on-screen color may lead you to believe otherwise, identically specified CMYK colors will match when they are printed.

The best way to predict how a CMYK color will look when printed is to use a printed reference—either a desktop color swatch book or a set of color swatch proofs printed from a file you have built yourself in a PostScript drawing program. (For more about getting predictable printed color, see "Calibrating Desktop Color" in Chapter 6.)

IT CAN TAKE MONTHS of reading manuals and experimenting to harness the power of PostScript illustration software. But a little insight into techniques used by others can save you a lot of time. The next four pages present some pointers for getting the most out of PostScript drawing programs.

LAYERED LINES The cloning feature of PostScript drawing programs, which makes a copy of the chosen object on top of the original, is handy for drawing patterned lines for maps and diagrams (16) or creating a glowing effect (17).

CUSTOM CLIP ART The ease of scaling PostScript art and its broad acceptance in page layout programs has given rise to many predrawn illustrations, or electronic *clip art*. With some simple PostScript manipulations, clip art can be customized for various applications (18).

18 Clip art supplied in PostScript format (immediately below) can be customized—for example, by filling the drawn shapes with color, cropping (above), copying, flipping or rotating.

16 A line with perfectly parallel stripes can be made from an original and several clones (copied exactly on top of the original). As each clone is made, a pattern, weight and color are assigned.

17 Blending between an original line (in this case the heavier, colored lines) and its clone can create a neon effect.

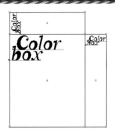

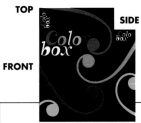

A PACKAGE LAYOUT By a series of scaling, rotating and skewing steps, a two-dimensional package layout can be turned into a three-dimensional mockup without using a 3D modeling program (19). Sometimes skewing can lead to rough corners where skewed lines meet. These can be repaired by changing the type of join assigned to the corner (20).

TRACING When you've imported a template for tracing, should you autotrace it or trace it by hand? Although autotracing functions have become increasingly sophisticated, the best choice still depends on the nature of the template (21). Some programs let you adjust the brightness and contrast of the template to enhance or suppress details for tracing by hand.

BLENDING TIPS A multistep blend can shape a color gradient around a curve (22). Blending can also help you develop a color palette (23).

19 This chart shows the steps used in Adobe Illustrator to create several common "3D" views from two-dimensional layouts. The order of the steps is all-important. The same metamorphosis can be accomplished in other PostScript illustration programs, although the angles of rotation may be expressed differently; for example, the sign of the angles may change. The steps shown here create the Trimetric view described in the chart. The box can be shown from other perspectives by designating different parts as the top, front and side.

		Axonometric		Isometric		Dimetric		Trimetric
TOP	Vert. scale	100.000%	Vert. scale	86.602%	Vert. scale	96.592%	Vert. scale	70.711%
	Horiz. shear	0°	Horiz. shear	30°	Horiz. shear	15°	Horiz. shear	45°
	Rotate	−45°	Rotate	−30°	Rotate	−15°	Rotate	−15°
FRONT	Vert. scale	70.7111%	Vert. scale	86.602%	Vert. scale	96.592%	Vert. scale	96.592%
	Horiz. shear	−45°	Horiz. shear	−30°	Horiz. shear	−15°	Horiz. shear	−15°
	Rotate	−45°	Rotate	−30°	Rotate	−15°	Rotate	−15°
SIDE	Vert. scale	70.711%	Vert. scale	86.602%	Vert. scale	50.000%	Vert. scale	86.602%
	Horiz. shear	45°	Horiz. shear	30°	Horiz. shear	60°	Horiz. shear	30°
	Rotate	45°	Rotate	30°	Rotate	60°	Rotate	30°

SCALE — TOP — 1
FRONT — 4
SIDE — 7
SKEW — 2
5
8
ROTATE — 3
6
9

EFFICIENT OUTPUT You can speed up the handling and printing of a PostScript-based illustration by cutting down on the amount of processing (or calculation) the output device has to do to carry out the PostScript instructions. Here are some tips for making drawings that are easy to work with and that print smoothly and quickly. Some PostScript drawing programs let you choose to have the software provide some of these services automatically.

• Group items together so they can be moved or transformed without having their parts knocked out of place.

• If your PostScript drawing program allows it, name your colors and line and fill styles, and then assign them to objects by name. That way if you change a color or pattern, you can alter it quickly and universally by changing the composition of the named color or line. Otherwise, you might have to select each object and assign its characteristics anew.

21 In general, autotracing works well for retaining a lot of fine detail in the bitmap being outlined (below) or for creating a special look from a scanned sketch. For creating smooth curves, it works better to place individual points by hand (left).

20 Rough corners that can occur when shapes are skewed (top) can be smoothed by joining the lines and assigning a rounded join style (bottom).

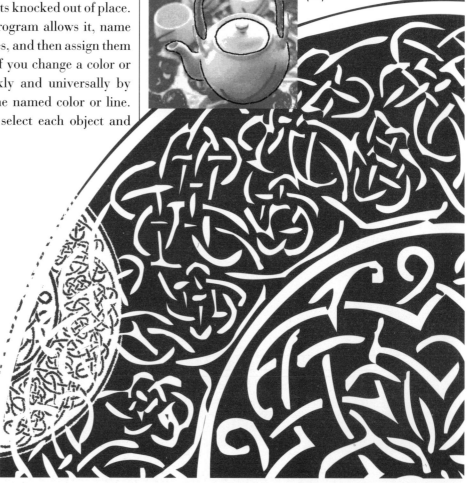

22 The secret of blending around a curve is to make the starting and ending points of the several blends perpendicular to the curve where they cross it (top). Using several steps can make a single-color curved blend (middle) or a multicolored one. Blends usually have to be masked to keep the color within the curved shape (bottom).

• Smooth curves are important, but there's no point in making them smoother than the eye can detect. *Flatness* is a measure of how much a path is allowed to deviate from the best curve the output device (printer or imagesetter) can make, with 0 being the tightest fit possible. For high-resolution output (see Chapter 6), a flatness setting of 3 or 4 typically speeds up output without deteriorating the image.

• *Rasterization* is the process of turning a PostScript image into the best possible pattern of dots that a particular monitor can display, a printer can print, or an imagesetter can produce on film. Blending, masking and using patterned fills require a lot of calculation on the part of the software that does the rasterization. Overusing these features in an illustration can lead to long waits for screen redraw or output.

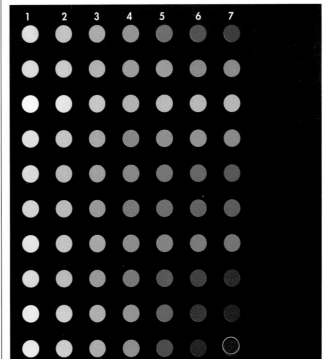

23 Some projects call for a palette of colors that will ensure an underlying consistency in a series of matching illustrations. The blend function of a PostScript drawing program can help create a range of colors for shading and three-dimensional effects. For each hue, begin by filling a circle with the most saturated color (shown here in column 7). Then clone the circle, drag it to the left and change its fill to the palest color (shown in column 1). Next make an intermediate, the "grayest" color (shown in column 4). To create two additional colors between the intermediate and each of the endpoints, use the blending function twice: First use the color spots in columns 1 and 4 as endpoints for blending in two steps (the colors in columns 2 and 3); then make another two-step blend using colors 4 and 7 (to get the colors in columns 5 and 6).

WHEN A COLOR IMAGE is printed, tiny shifts of the paper on the press can produce gaps in ink coverage that allow the white of the paper to show through (24). For traditional artwork, the specialists who prepare the film to make printing plates use photographic methods of spreading abutting colors into each other to prevent white gaps. This process is called *trapping*. With digital separation methods, trapping is built into the artwork files before film separations are output. Trapping is much more often required in object-oriented artwork, which consists of distinct drawn objects, than in pixel-based, or continuous-tone images, where the color areas tend to blend continuously into one another.

CHOKE AND SPREAD *Spreading* is enlarging one object so that it slightly overlaps an adjacent one. *Choking* is slightly reducing the size of the *knockout* that's formed in the background so that the color of a foreground object can print clearly, without mixing with the background color. Like the spread, the choke causes an overlap (25). Whether to choke or spread depends largely on the characteristics of the artwork. In general, it's best to expand a lighter color into a darker one rather than vice versa (26).

In PostScript illustration, choking or spreading of graphic objects or type is often accomplished by overprinting the stroke but not the fill (27). Overprinting makes the stroke print on top of anything that's behind it, rather than printing on blank paper. An alternative to overprinting is to use a stroke that's a mixture of the two abutting colors (28). Some PostScript programs provide special trapping functions. The trapping algorithm analyzes the color composition of abutting objects and draws the trapping strokes needed (29).

WHEN AND HOW MUCH TO TRAP Whether and how much to trap depends on the characteristics of the artwork and how the piece will be printed—that is, the kind of press, ink and paper that will be used. But there is some agreement among experienced printers and artists that a 0.25-point trap is a good starting point if these conditions are unknown when the artwork is designed. In most PostScript programs, half the stroke width extends inward from the edge of the fill and half extends outward. So, if colors are "self-trapped" with an overprinted stroke of the same color, the trapping stroke needs to be twice the width of the desired trap, because only half the stroke width extends into the second color. But if an overprinted stroke of a third color is used, the entire stroke width will act as a trap. Since information about press, ink and paper may not be available when artwork is being designed, the amount of trap may have to be changed later.

24 Ideally, as artwork is printed in two or more colors, all colors of ink are applied to the page in perfect registration; abutting colors neither overlap nor gap at the edges (top). In reality, however, as paper travels through the press, slight shifts in position often cause the different ink colors to be laid down slightly out of register (bottom).

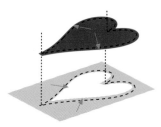

25 To prevent the white gaps that can occur with misregistration, ink colors can be made to trap to one another by spreading one color (enlarging an object slightly) (top) or choking another (reducing the size of the knockout provided for printing the first color) (bottom).

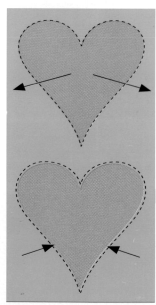

26 When a light color is spread into a darker in order to provide trapping (top), the overlap that occurs tends to distort the design less than if the dark color is expanded (bottom), visibly shrinking the size of the light object.

For some kinds of PostScript artwork, it may be better not to trap. For example, for artwork printed in pastel colors, a sliver of white might be preferable to a darker "outlined" look that could result from trapping.

If the artist doesn't build trapping into the file, either by hand or with a drawing program's automatic trapping function, it can still be applied in other ways. Some page layout programs trap more or less automatically, although they don't provide trapping inside the illustrations that have been imported from other programs. Some imagesetting service bureaus offer trapping services to artists who don't want to do it themselves. And special programs (for example, TrapWise) have been developed to trap all elements on the page as a file is being output on film.

TRAPPING TIPS Here are some hints for trapping object-oriented art:
• Trapping to black: A way to create a smooth, rich black and to trap a color against it as well is to use that color as a component of the black (30).
• Trapping reverse type: When you reverse type out of a rich black, you run the risk of having color show at the edges of the type. Adding a black stroke will effectively push any other colors in the black away from the edge of the type (31). But it will also reduce the weight of the white letter, which can make small type unreadable. A way to trap without changing the weight of the letters is to add a "process white" stroke. That is, add a stroke whose color is made up of 1 percent of each of the three process primaries—cyan, magenta and yellow. This stroke should *not* be set to overprint. The percentage of color in the stroke will be too small to show up in the half of the stroke width that extends into the white type, but it will effectively push the higher densities of the three primary colors in the black back away from the edges of the letters.
• Trapping by palette: By choosing a palette in which each color shares at least one primary component with every other color, you may be able to avoid the need to use overprinting strokes for trapping. If misregistration occurs on-press, no white gap appears because the shared components continue from one colored object to the next.

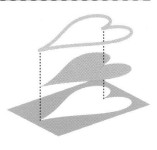

27 With a fill and an overprinted stroke of the same color, the knock-out in the second color allows the fill to print cleanly, while the overprinted stroke extends into the second color slightly to provide a margin of safety in case misregistration occurs.

28 Another way to trap is to overprint a stroke that is some mixture of the two abutting colors. In this case, since the two abutting colors are light, the amount of each color in the trapping stroke was reduced to half, so that the overlap wouldn't cause a dark border effect.

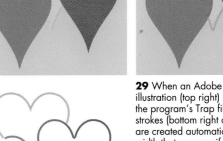

29 When an Adobe Illustrator illustration (top right) is treated with the program's Trap filter, trapping strokes (bottom right and below) are created automatically at the width that you specify.

31 Adding color to make a rich black (as in Figure 30) can cause a "halo" of color at the edges of white type if misregistration occurs on press. If the weight of the type is quite heavy relative to the trapping stroke, a black stroke can be added to solve the problem (far left). The black stroke knocks out of the color, to effectively push color away from the reversed-out type (left). Because the stroke is very thin, the difference between the black of the stroke and the rich black of the background isn't seen.

30 When a brightly colored object appears against a black background, white gaps can be especially apparent if misregistration occurs, because of the stark contrast between the bright color, the black and the white (left). To trap the object, the color can be mixed into the black to make the black look richer and to prevent white gaps from occurring in case of misregistration (right).

5

Pixel-Based Artwork

Painting and Photorealistic Color

Preparing a Scanned Photo for Print

Tips for Painting and Image Editing

WHEN COLOR MADE ITS WAY to the desktop, early bitmapped painting and photo-editing software evolved into sophisticated painting and image-processing programs that now overlap in their functions. In many programs it's hard to separate the freely artistic painting functions from the photorealistic image-editing capabilities (1).

PAINTING Color painting programs imitate natural media—painting with oils or watercolors, or drawing with pen, pencil, charcoal or pastels, for example (2). The toolkits of bitmapped painting programs typically include a paintbrush (for soft-edged strokes), a pencil (for sharp, well-defined, hard-edged line work), a paint bucket or Fill function (for flooding spaces with color), an eraser (for removing paint to reveal the background color), an eyedropper tool (for sampling color from an image in order to paint with it or add it to the palette), a "cloning" tool (for repeating an element, pattern or texture) and selection tools (for cutting and pasting parts of the picture).

PHOTOREALISTIC COLOR Color image-editing software can correct, enhance or combine scanned images, primarily photographs. Typically, image-editing software can
- Accept images recorded with either high-end scanning equipment or a desktop scanner (see Chapter 3).
- Correct the color balance of an entire image or a selected part of it (3).
- Adjust brightness and contrast.
- Sharpen or soften the appearance of an image (4).
- Retouch flaws or remove elements from a photo (5).
- Isolate areas of an image to expose or protect them from effects (6).
- Scale, crop, rotate or distort the perspective of an image or some component of it.
- Make composites by combining parts of several images, adjusting the transparency of each component and smoothing and blending the edges for a seamless join (see "Combining Images" on page 50).

1 This image, created with the ColorStudio image-editing program, seamlessly combines digitally painted elements (the elephants) with a photographic image (the sky with clouds).

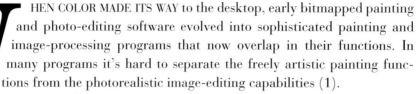

2 Fractal Design Painter provides a toolkit of pens, brushes, pencils and chalk. In addition, it supplies several paper textures that can be applied to an image while it's being painted or after it's complete. Using a pressure-sensitive digitizing tablet with the painting software enhances the feeling of working with natural media.

3 Good color balance depends on the proper ratio of primary colors in neutral areas. An image that is not balanced shows a *color cast,* an unwanted overabundance of one hue. A red cast in the midtones (those colors between the light highlights and the dark shadows) (left) was removed from this image (right) by reducing the magenta and yellow components with Adobe Photoshop's Color Balance controls.

4 An image whose focus is not sharp can be improved by applying special algorithms, or filters, built into image-editing software. The appearance of an image that was slightly out of focus (left) was improved by applying Photoshop's Sharpen More filter (right). Another filter that sharpens images is Unsharp Mask. (See "Sharpening" on page 52.)

5 Photoshop's rubber stamp tool can copy the color and texture from one area of an image and apply it elsewhere. This technique provides a good start for hiding blemishes or removing unwanted parts of a scanned photo. For this portrait, other people in the image were removed by cloning grass from the background.

6 The house in this image (top) was selected, and a mask was made (middle) to protect it from changing color when the saturation was increased to intensify the color of the lawn, hills and sky (bottom).

7 The photo at upper left was the original image. It has been treated with three special-effects filters (clockwise): The Chalk & Charcoal filter from Gallery Effects, a library of artistic effects that can be applied to color bitmaps; the Find Edges filter from Photoshop, and Poster Edges, another Gallery Effects filter. Although they can be applied to any image, these effects can be particularly helpful for adding interest to a rather ordinary-looking photo. Like the filters used with some PostScript illustration programs, filters used with pixel-based software are "miniprograms." They automate a variety of color-correction tasks and special effects.

• Create special effects—for example, to achieve a particular artistic treatment for an image (7) or to improve the look of a less-than-perfect photo.

• Silhouette part of an image for importing into a page layout program (8).

• Convert from RGB color (the native color format of many scanned and painted images) to CMYK color for desktop color separations.

ADJUSTING COLOR Many image-editing programs include graphs—a histogram and a set of curves. The artist can modify the brightness, contrast and color balance of an image by making changes to these graphs. The histogram shows how many pixels of each tone, shade or hue occur in an image (9). The curves map the relationship between data stored in the image file and altered data stored in a corrected image on-screen. By knowing what the curves represent, the artist can use them to preview the results of planned changes to an image before saving the changes as permanent modifications of the file (10).

SCALING PIXEL-BASED IMAGES Unlike Post-Script drawings, which can be scaled up or down without any loss of detail or precision, pixel-based images can lose information in the scaling process. When the size of a pixel-based image is reduced, the software has more information than it needs to specify the colors of the decreased number of pixels; the software throws away the excess information from the image at its original size. Conversely, when an image is enlarged, the software has to invent additional color data for the new pixels that are added to the image. Although some programs are good at these interpolation processes, too much enlargement means too much made-up color data, and the image begins to deteriorate (11).

8 Photoshop's pen tool allows the artist to draw a silhouetting outline, or *clipping path* (top), that will automatically silhouette the image when it's placed in a page layout document (bottom).

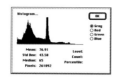

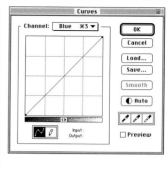

9 The histograms for these two scanned photos show the brightness levels within the images. For each brightness level along the horizontal axis, the height of the graph tells how many pixels have that particular brightness. In the image at the left, many pixels fall into the darkest and lightest brightness levels; in the image on the right, there are fewer pixels at the extremes of the range, with two peaks in the midtones.

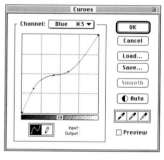

10 By manipulating curves in Photoshop, the artist can change the relative amounts of detail that appear in highlight, midtone and shadow portions of the tonal range of an image. A straight line at a 45-degree angle means that tones displayed on-screen are the same as those recorded in the image file (top). Changing the curve so that some parts are steep and others are flat results in a change in the distribution of tones (bottom).

11 When a pixel-based image is reduced in size, some information is thrown away, but we don't necessarily notice the loss of information because the size reduction makes *all* the detail in the picture harder to see. On the other hand, when an image is enlarged too much, the software can't successfully fill in the missing data it needs for the additional pixels, so we perceive a loss of quality.

12 To make this photomontage (lower right), several scanned elements were pasted into and pasted behind the hands of the clock. Photoshop's compositing functions were used to control which colors in the clock image were protected and which could be replaced by pixels from the pasted elements.

COMBINING IMAGES Photomontage is one of the most popular uses for image-editing software. Sophisticated selecting, cutting and pasting tools make it possible to isolate parts of several images and combine them (12). If you save a mask for a selected element, you can select exactly that portion of the image again and alter it without changing other parts of the picture (13). A recently added feature of some pixel-based programs is the ability to work with elements of a montage as if they were transparent layers of acetate, rearranging parts of the composite by sliding the layers around

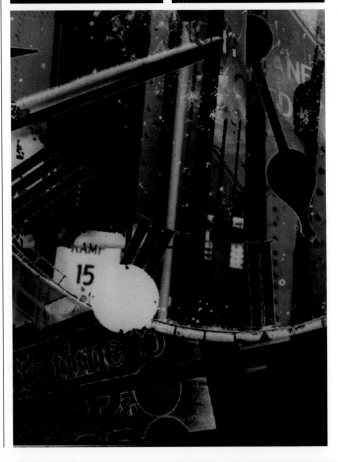

13 This selection mask (middle) makes it possible to isolate the hummingbird shape in this Photoshop montage, so that its color can be manipulated without changing other parts of the image.

without disturbing the pixels underneath (14).

SMOOTHING EDGES, HIDING SEAMS The human eye is an expert detector of edges. For instance, it can see the stairstepping of square pixels in a slanted line or the edge of one photo element in a composite. To visually smooth out the stairstepping, color image-editing software uses a process called *antialiasing* (15). *Feathering*, a fading of one image into another around the edges, can also be used to blend the edges of one part of an image into another part (16).

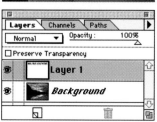

14 Photoshop allows you to treat elements as objects, moving and rearranging them on separate layers without disturbing the pixels underneath. (Compare this relatively new feature of pixel-based programs with the basic construction of color bitmaps illustrated in Figure 11 of Chapter 2, on page 16.)

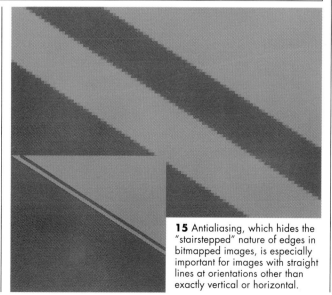

15 Antialiasing, which hides the "stairstepped" nature of edges in bitmapped images, is especially important for images with straight lines at orientations other than exactly vertical or horizontal.

16 Feathering can be used to select a part of an image to be modified and pasted back into the original. For example, when the girls' faces were selected from this image (top) for color correction of the skin tones, feathering was applied (middle) so that the altered selection would blend with the original colors in the hair (bottom).

ALL SCANNED PHOTOS CAN BENEFIT from certain kinds of image editing before printing. For scans done on high-end equipment by color-separation experts, these corrections are often made at the time of scanning. But for desktop scans they are typically made with an image-editing program. Even the best scans usually need sharpening, adjustment of the tonal range, and conversion from RGB to CMYK color.

SHARPENING The sampling processes used by scanners (described in Chapter 3) introduce a certain amount of "fuzziness" as the scan is made—the scanned image is not as sharp as the original image recorded on film. For high-end scans, sharpening (along with other corrections) is usually done before the scan files are delivered to you. The kind and degree of corrections are based on information you provide about how the image will be used.

For desktop scanners, corrections must usually be made with Adobe Photoshop or another image-editing program. This is also true of the scan files provided on Kodak Photo CD discs, which are usually written to Photo CD without the scan operator knowing how they will be used and thus what corrections are appropriate.

Although several sharpening routines are provided by image-editing software, some are generally better than others for correcting the fuzziness introduced by scanning. The goal of sharpening is to increase the contrast between areas of distinctly different colors without increasing the differences between pixels that vary only slightly in color. For this purpose, *unsharp masking* is often the most effective sharpening procedure. For example, unsharp masking will increase the contrast between the pupil, iris and white of an eye (and thus appear to bring them into sharper focus) without speckling the skin by sharpening the subtle color differences in the flesh tones of the face (17, 18).

Going by the Numbers

Even in a calibrated desktop color system (see "Calibrating Desktop Color" on page 66), the color transmitted by a computer screen can never look exactly the same as the color reflected from the printed page. In PostScript illustration programs, colors can be mixed by the artist using specified percentages of cyan, magenta, yellow and black. But the continuous-tone photos edited in pixel-based programs include many more colors, and they are not mixed by the artist.

To help you predict how printed color will look, image-editing programs such as Adobe Photoshop have sampling tools for determining the CMYK composition of color at any point in an image. You can use Photoshop's eyedropper tool to locate the point to be sampled and then read the CMYK composition displayed in the Info window to see how the color will be separated for printing. (The percentages listed in the Info window will depend on the program's current settings for color separation; see "Converting from RGB to CMYK" on page 53.)

To really benefit from using the color sampling tools of either PostScript or pixel-based graphics software, you'll need a printed color reference, with color swatches labeled with their CMYK composition. You can buy a desktop color swatch book (such as Agfa's *PostScript Process Color Guide*) or make your own swatch files and have color proofs made. Once you gain some experience using sampling tools and a printed color chart, you'll be able to look at CMYK percentages and envision how the sampled color will look when it's printed.

ADJUSTING THE RANGE OF TONES The *tonal range*, or *range of tones*, in an image is the brightness difference between the lightest color and the darkest color. As described in Chapter 1, the range of tones that can be reproduced with ink on paper is smaller than the range that can be recorded on film. So a slide or a negative that uses the full color range of the film it's recorded on will necessarily have its color range compressed when it's printed on a press.

Typically, the maximum range of tones that can be printed with CMYK inks is only about two-thirds of the maximum range of tones of a scanned slide or negative. That means, for instance, that for every three tones on the film, only two tones will show up in print. But with image-editing software, you can control where in the color range the tonal loss takes place, so that images with the most detail in the highlights (lightest colors), the midtones or the shadows (darkest colors) can retain much of their detail.

CONVERTING FROM RGB TO CMYK To print an image with ink on paper, it must be converted from the RGB color gamut of film and scans to the more restricted CMYK process printing gamut. But when and how should the conversion be made?

When To Convert Artists who work with pixel-based programs on the desktop differ in their opinions about whether to make the RGB-to-CMYK conversion early or late in the image-editing or painting process. On the one hand, converting early lets you see, as you work, a better representation of the colors that will eventually print. But some artists like working in the larger, brighter RGB gamut to develop the image with the best-looking color they can achieve, then convert the image to CMYK. If the converted color is too dull or drab, they can use the tonal range, hue and saturation controls to restore as much vividness as possible.

ORIGINAL PHOTO: DIGITAL STOCK, SOLANA BEACH, CA

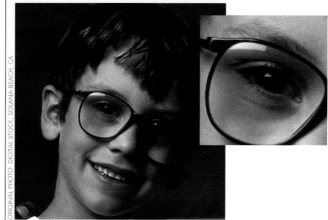

17 When a scanned photo (top) is treated with Photoshop's Unsharp Mask filter, the software looks at the color differences in the image and then increases the difference (sharpens) if the adjacent pixels were already quite different, as in the eyes in this portrait. On the other hand, in areas where the pixels are quite similar in color to begin with, no increase in contrast is applied, as in the subtle variations in the skin tones of the face.

18 The KPT Sharpen Intensity filter from the Kai's Power Tools set of filters for Photoshop applies unsharp masking and adjusts the tonal range of the image at the same time, as you can see by comparing the two versions of this image, shown before (top) and after (bottom) the application of the filter.

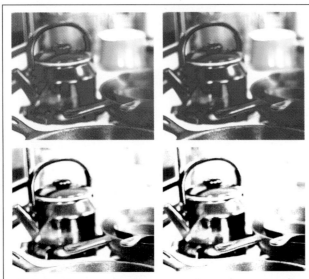

19 Undercolor removal replaces cyan, yellow and magenta with black in dark and neutral areas. This image is shown as it was separated in Photoshop with (left) and without (right) undercolor removal. In each case the black separation is shown on the bottom, and a combined printing of the cyan, magenta and yellow plates is shown above it.

The choice of whether to convert early or late may depend on the kind of image you're developing. If the goal is simply to prepare a scanned photo for print, converting early may be the better choice. However, if the image involves quite a bit of painting, photomontage or special-effects treatment, you may want to convert later.

How Conversion Works When an image is converted from the RGB to the CMYK color system, the software can choose from many different ways to make the conversion. That's because in the CMYK system, dark areas can be represented by black ink or by a mixture of cyan, magenta and yellow inks. In most cases dark areas are reproduced by using all four colors of ink. As explained later in this section, there are advantages to increasing or decreasing the amount of black in the mix.

The sophistication of the software in representing black has been one of the distinguishing features between desktop color correction and the expert work done with more expensive machinery at high-end color-separation houses. One of the goals in deciding how to represent black is to get a true black rather than a muddy gray-brown. Another aim is to not put more ink on the press than it can successfully print on the paper. (A rule of thumb used by many printers is to limit total coverage [C, M, Y and K percentages added together] to somewhere between 260 and 300 percent. Too much ink will smear and won't dry properly, filling in details in the image. A third goal is to avoid an abrupt shift from light to dark shades of color.

Three important *black-generation* functions that image-editing software performs automatically or under the control of the artist are undercolor removal (UCR), gray component replacement (GCR) and undercolor addition (UCA). *Undercolor removal* is the replacement of cyan, magenta and yellow components with black ink in the shadow tones of an image (19).

Gray component replacement is the substitution of black ink for the cyan, magenta and yellow mixture that makes up the graying (or achromatic) component of any color. Because it takes less black to darken a color than it would take cyan, magenta or yellow or some combination of these colors, the overall ink coverage is reduced. Another advantage of using GCR is that it tends to make neutral tones more stable. It allows the printer to increase or decrease the ink coverage of cyan, magenta or yellow on the press to

20 Gray component replacement cuts down on the amount of ink used on the press. Typically, only a part of the neutralizing color is removed. Separations for these two versions of the same image were produced with Photoshop's light (left) and heavy (right) black-generation settings. In each case the black plate that resulted is shown on the bottom, and the entire composite image is shown on the top.

correct the way a particular part of an image is printing, without introducing a color cast to neutral areas elsewhere in the image. For example, if flesh tones appear too red in a particular photo, the amount of red applied by the press can be reduced without worrying too much about whether areas of neutral color elsewhere in the picture will change color as a result (20).

One disadvantage that can arise from UCR or GCR is an abrupt break between light and dark areas of complex colors like flesh tones. Another problem is that blacks printed with black ink alone can look too "thin." *Undercolor addition* is a way some image-editing programs compensate for taking out too much color from dark or neutral areas when UCR or GCR is carried out. For instance, adding cyan, magenta and yellow to the shadow tones can increase the depth of the shadows. And if relatively large areas of dense black coverage are needed, it's helpful to add back some cyan, magenta and yellow to increase the richness and coverage of the dark color (21).

Getting the best results from UCR, GCR and UCA depends not only on the nature of the image, but also on the press, paper and ink that will be used to print it. Before deciding to set UCR, GCR or UCA at levels other than those set automatically by scanning and image-editing software, it's a good idea to consult the printer.

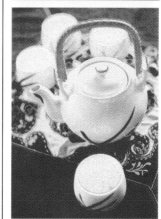

21 If too much color is removed when UCR or GCR is applied, large areas of black can look "thin" or uneven. Adding back some color improves ink coverage in such areas. Shown here are composite cyan, magenta and yellow plates for 0% (middle) and 50% (bottom) undercolor addition in Photoshop. The entire image, including the black plate and without undercolor addition, is shown at the top.

THE PAINTING AND IMAGE-EDITING capabilities of color bitmap or pixel-based software can be effectively combined with PostScript drawing. In addition, color image-editing programs can be put to work to produce specialized color treatments of black-and-white photos.

COMBINING POSTSCRIPT AND BITMAPS Several painting/image-editing programs can import PostScript art. This allows the artist to bring artwork created with the technically precise interface of PostScript drawing programs into the bitmap environment (22, 23). Some bitmapped programs even provide a PostScript adjunct to provide both drawing and painting/image-editing functions in a single program. Going the other direction, from pixel-based software into a PostScript-based drawing program, we've already seen that bitmaps can be imported into PostScript programs as nonprinting templates for tracing. It's also possible to incorporate pixel-based art so that it prints as part of a PostScript file.

BETTER BLENDS Many painting and image-editing programs can produce gradations somewhat like those described in Chapter 4 for PostScript illustration programs. But the blends created in bitmapped programs can be modified to look softer, rougher or less precise and mechanical than PostScript gradations.

DUOTONES, TRITONES AND QUADTONES *Duotones* are two-color halftone prints of black-and-white photos. In most duotones black serves as the primary ink. The second color may also be black or gray, used to extend the range of shades and tones beyond what a single printing of black ink can accomplish. Alternatively a subtle second color may warm or cool the image (24), or a more intense hue may add dramatic impact (25) or integrate the photo into the overall color scheme of a printed piece. To make a duotone, an image-editing program produces two versions of an image, each of which can be manipulated separately, to vary each color's contribution to the overall effect. The artist can regulate how each color is used in the highlights, midtones and shadows.

Tritones and *quadtones* are three- and four-color halftone reproductions. Like duotones, they can be used to produce subtle (26) or dramatic (27) color effects. Duotones, tritones and quadtones are often produced with black ink and custom inks such as Pantone colors. But they can also be printed with two to four of the CMYK process inks. (Color-separating a duotone, tritone or quadtone as part of a page can be tricky. You'll need to know the best file format for saving the image file in order to ensure that your page layout program has the color separation information it needs. A good imagesetting service bureau—see "Working with a Service Bureau" in Chapter 6—or the technical support group for the image-editing or page layout software should be able to help.)

22 It's possible to combine the technical precision of PostScript illustration and typesetting with the image-editing capabilities of color painting and image-editing programs. The nail polish bottle was drawn and colored in Adobe Illustrator and then imported into Photoshop, where highlights, shadows and tones were added.

23 The image of Abraham Automotives was "sketched" in Illustrator. That is, the straight lines of the building were drawn, type was set for the signage, and the parts of the image that would benefit from precise, repeated operations such as cloning or rotating were drawn. Then the drawing was imported into Photoshop, where all color was added, including blends to create the natural lighting on the walls of the buildings.

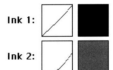

24 A typical use of the second color in a duotone is to add to the range of tones available for the shadows or to "cool" the image by adding a blue tint (as shown here), or to "warm" it by adding a red. The graphs show that the black in this duotone has been changed very little (in the unaltered grayscale image, the curve would show a straight line at 45 degrees, from the highlights at the lower left to the shadows at the upper right). The graph for the blue shows that very little color has been added in the highlights and midtones (the curve is flat at the lower left); color has been added mainly in the upper midtones and shadow range (lower).

Ink 1:

Ink 2:

26 In this tritone, adding magenta and yellow, especially to the shadows, deepens the range of tones and "warms" the image.

Ink 1:

Ink 2:

Ink 3:

25 In this duotone the use of the blue has been expanded into the highlights and midtones (making the blue curve steeper on the left) and reduced in the shadows (flattening the curve on the right). Black has been reduced in the highlights and lighter midtones. The overall effect is to "color" the image. This kind of duotone could be used, for example, to pick up the second color in a two-color page.

Ink 1:

Ink 2:

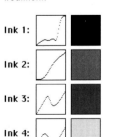

27 "Wildly" manipulating the colors of a quadtone can produce a very colorful photo treatment.

Ink 1:

Ink 2:

Ink 3:

Ink 4:

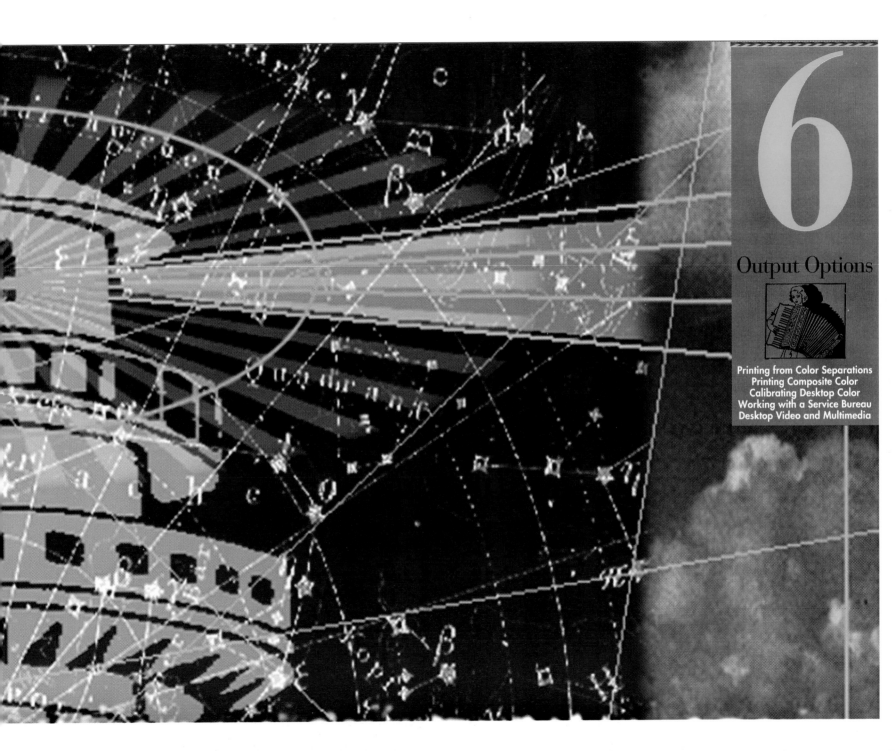

ALTHOUGH DESKTOP COMPOSITE COLOR PRINTING is ideal for some kinds of publications, the most commonly used method of producing printed pages from desktop artwork is to produce digitally separated film, from which printing plates are made. Because the imagesetting equipment that makes these separations is complex and relatively expensive, film is often produced by *imagesetting service bureaus*, businesses specially equipped to accept desktop color files and deliver separated film. (See "Working with a Service Bureau" on page 68.)

TRADITIONAL AND DIGITAL METHODS In traditional methods of producing printed materials, a publication is designed and then a design comp is produced for approval before further work is done. When the design has been approved, type and illustrations are pasted up to execute the design on artboards. Then these *mechanicals* are photographed or color separated, if need be, to generate the film from which printing plates are made. Color photos are also separated and assigned *halftone screens*, dot patterns for applying the four process ink colors so images on the pages will reproduce clearly. In making the final film by traditional methods, film-preparation professionals may have to make one or more sets of duplicate or composite negatives—to put parts of a page together or to trap images, for example. (For further discussion of this topic, see "Trapping" on page 42.) From this film, proofing prints can be generated so color can be assessed before the printing plates are made (1).

As we've seen in the last several chapters, with desktop methods, the page composition, typesetting and even color-correction and separation tasks can be done on the computer, so film can be output as full pages without the need for hand compositing. Comps and even certain kinds of proofs can be made directly from the electronic file, saving the expense of making film and a final film-based proof until all last-minute changes have been made.

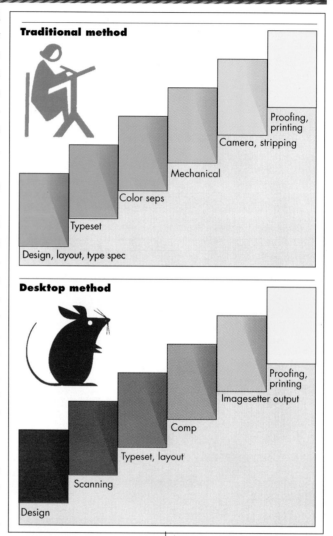

Traditional method

Design, layout, type spec — Typeset — Color seps — Mechanical — Camera, stripping — Proofing, printing

Desktop method

Design — Scanning — Typeset, layout — Comp — Imagesetter output — Proofing, printing

1 In the traditional prepress process, mechanical layouts are assembled from separate type and line art, and spaces are provided for color separations. The mechanical is photographed, the film for all the elements is stripped together and printing plates are made. With fully digital desktop processes, pages can be assembled and stripped electronically and output as final film or even as printing plates.

What's Black-and-White and Read All Over?

Even though beautiful color is the goal, black-and-white laser prints are still all-important for publications sent to an imagesetting service bureau for output, as described on the next two pages. For large printing projects, the cost of printing color-composite printer's dummies using any of the methods described on pages 64–65 may not be cost-effective. Low-cost black-and-white laser prints can work very well to show where images should appear and how color pages should separate.

But color adds a great deal to the page, even for working proofs. A compromise between cost and color is to print full-size dummy pages as both composites and separations on a black-and-white laser printer and also print color thumbnails with one or two spreads per page. This combination cuts the cost by cutting the total number of color pages, but it still provides all the layout and separation information the designer and service bureau need.

HOW IMAGESETTERS WORK Regardless of what kind of information is stored in an electronic file—type, object-oriented graphics or continuous-tone images—when it's time to color-separate and output the file, that information has to be translated into device-specific dot patterns that the imagesetter can produce on film (2). If the file is stored in the PostScript page-description language (which has become the standard for desktop color work) and output as halftone separations, there are two elements that go into the dot pattern: the output resolution and the halftone resolution, or screen ruling. Both are important components of the PostScript halftoning process. (See "Resolution" in Chapter 3.)

POSTSCRIPT HALFTONES In PostScript-based halftone output, each halftone cell can contain a number of tinier imagesetter dots. The more imagesetter dots a halftone cell can hold, the more different sizes of halftone dots the device can produce (3). Since each different size of halftone dot means a different level of color in a separation (or a different level of gray in a black-and-white image), the more dot sizes, the more different colors you can print.

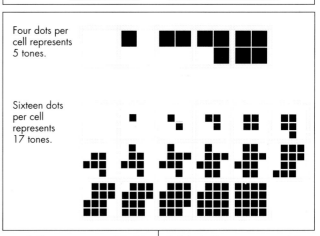

2 In a PostScript-based imagesetter, the raster image processor (or RIP) translates instructions written in the PostScript language into a dot pattern for each of the four process colors. The recorder then uses a laser beam to image these dot patterns on film.

Data file

Raster image processor (RIP)

Imagesetter

Processor

Film or paper

Four dots per cell represents 5 tones.

Sixteen dots per cell represents 17 tones.

3 If the halftone screen resolution (lpi) is held constant, increasing the output resolution (dpi) results in more dots per halftone cell. This allows more variation in the sizes of halftone dots, and thus more different tones can be produced in film output.

4 At a halftone screen ruling of 100 lpi (left), the individual halftone dots can be seen, interfering with the illusion of a continuous-tone image. At a screen ruling of 150 lpi (right), the dots are not perceptible without a magnifier.

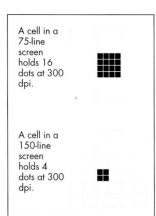

A cell in a 75-line screen holds 16 dots at 300 dpi.

A cell in a 150-line screen holds 4 dots at 300 dpi.

5 In some cases output resolution (dpi) may have to be held constant—for instance, because the choice of output devices is limited. Because of the relationship between output resolution and halftone screen resolution, this may in turn limit the number of tones that can be printed. As the halftone screen ruling increases, the number of output dots per halftone cell decreases, and therefore the variety of halftone dot sizes decreases also.

At low screen rulings, an image can look coarse because the individual halftone dots are perceptible (4). To eliminate the perception of dots, we can increase the number of halftone cells per inch—that is, increase the screen density. Color and grayscale images in printed material are usually printed with screens of 120, 133 or 150 lines per inch, sometimes even 200 or more. But you can see that if you increase the screen ruling but keep the output resolution the same, the number of dots available for each halftone cell decreases. So the number of different color levels goes down (5). To optimize the appearance of an image, you have to balance the line screen ruling and the number of output dots per inch (6).

MOIRÉ Over the short history of imagesetting with PostScript, one of the major concerns about the quality of the final product has involved *moiré*, an obvious pattern that can occur on the printed page when halftone dot screens in the four process colors are overlaid (7). To avoid this obvious patterning, the traditional angles and screen rulings for generating halftone screens have been modified in various ways by different manufacturers of imagesetting equipment. Some imagesetting equipment can even vary the size of the tiny dots that make up a halftone screen dot, which improves the shape of the halftone dot and helps avoid moiré.

STOCHASTIC SCREENING Even if the halftone patterning is not apparent as a visible moiré, it does tend to "soften" an image by interfering with sharp definition of the breaks between contrasting colors. Instead of being crisp, the edges of the color breaks are made slightly fuzzy by the halftoning pattern. To solve the moiré problem and increase overall sharpness, some imagesetting equipment uses stochastic screening instead of halftone screening.

In stochastic screening, the dot size doesn't vary as it does in halftone screening. Instead, all the dots are uniformly tiny, and differences in color are produced by varying the density of the dots, clumping many dots together or spreading fewer dots wider apart. A dense clumping of dots produces intense color; widely dispersed dots make pale colors; intermediate densities make the colors in between.

The dots in stochastic screening are not placed in lines as in halftone screening. Rather, their placement is somewhat randomized. Since no screening angles are used, no uniform dot pattern develops. This eliminates the possibility of moiré and also the slight fuzziness typically introduced by digital halftone screening.

Images printed from film produced with stochastic screening tend to be darker and to show higher contrast than those produced from the same files with standard PostScript halftoning. If you're accustomed to digital halftone color separations, you may have to make adjustments to the color in your files to get the results you expect from the stochastic screening process.

Output Resolution (DPI)	Screen Frequency (LPI)								
	53	60	75	85	100	120	133	150	200
300	33	26	17						
600		101	65	51	37				
1200		401»256	257»256	200	145	101			
1270			287»256	224	162	113	92		
2400				798»256	577»256	401»256	327»256	257»256	145
2540					649»256	451»256	393»256	289»256	163
3600								577»256	324»256

CORRECTING FOR PRESS CONDITIONS In making final film and plates for printing, planning for characteristics of the press, ink and paper becomes very important. The precision of the press in *registering* the page as each color of ink is applied determines the need for trapping.

Dot gain also has to be considered. As a page runs through the press, the dots of ink that go onto the paper may not be exactly the same size as the dots that were imaged on the film from which printing plates were made. Dot gain is an increase in dot size due in part to the nature of the ink and the absorbency of the paper. It can increase color intensity by putting more ink on the page than was called for by the digital information in the original artwork file (8). Some graphics programs have built-in functions that change the artwork to counteract the dot gain that will occur on-press. With other programs, it's up to the artist to compensate by lightening the colors used in the image.

OTHER OUTPUT OPTIONS Besides composite color prints (see page 64) and output through an imagesetting service bureau, desktop color files can also be produced on "high-end" color separation systems. Desktop computer–based systems can be linked to more expensive proprietary systems such as those of Scitex and Linotype-Hell, for example, for separation by experienced color-separation professionals.

Another option is to output a digital color file to a *film recorder*. In this case the digital information in the file is used to expose film to red, green and blue light to re-create the image as a transparency. Film recorders can be used to make 35mm slides for presentation, for example, or 4 x 5-inch or 8 x 10-inch transparencies for reproduction. For print reproduction, the transparencies can be color-separated with photographic or high-end digital methods to make film separations and printing plates. (Although it may seem a bit counterproductive to go from a desktop digital file to a film transparency and then to traditional color separation, this process can be useful for specialized kinds of printing that don't accept digital files as input.)

Additional output options—especially for animated color productions—are videotape and multimedia (see "Desktop Video and Multimedia" on page 72).

6 The maximum number of levels of color available in output from a PostScript halftone imagesetter can be calculated for a given line screen and output resolution as follows:

Number of levels = $(dpi/lpi)^2 + 1$

This chart shows the number of levels of color available in each separation for various standard output resolutions and line screens, based on the equation shown. Consulting the chart can tell you what output resolution to use if you'll be printing in a publication that requires a certain halftone screen: Choose the lowest output resolution you can without going under a value of 256 levels. Or, if you are limited to a particular output resolution but have a choice of screen rulings, it can help you figure out how high your screen ruling can be. Recall that the nature of PostScript limits the number of different shades that can be expressed to 256. So if the calculated value is higher than 256, the real value is 256.

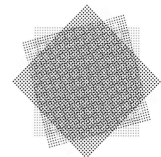

7 A *moiré* is an obvious, unwanted pattern generated by interference caused by the interaction between the halftone screens of the four colors used in process color printing.

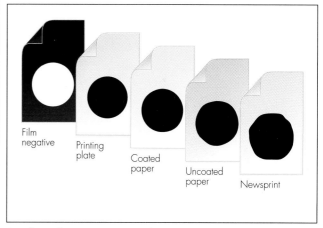

Film negative

Printing plate

Coated paper

Uncoated paper

Newsprint

8 Halftone dots can increase or decrease in size between the time they are recorded on film by the imagesetter and when they are printed on paper. In general, the nature of the materials and processes used in platemaking and printing result in an overall increase in dot size, called *dot gain*.

DEVELOPING IN PARALLEL WITH DESKTOP COLOR design and production methods have been new ways to print color pages (9). Instead of using printing plates on a press to put ink on paper, these new technologies produce color pages in other ways, opening up possibilities for color print projects that require relatively few copies and have budgets that wouldn't otherwise allow for color (see "Choosing a Printing Process" on this page). In addition, short-run color printers can be used early in the development of a project to produce *design comps*, or *comprehensive sketches*, that look very much like the final printed piece.

Short-run color printers can be categorized by the kind of technology they use to make the print and by whether they are PostScript-driven. Some color printers are priced low enough so they can relatively easily become part of the desktop equipment in a design studio. Others are usually found in photocopying or imagesetting service bureaus. Short-run color printers are typically low-resolution devices, putting 200 to 600 dots per inch on the page, compared to medium-resolution devices at 1000 to 1600 dots per inch and high-resolution imagesetters that produce film at 2000 to 3600 dots or more per inch for traditional printing processes.

COLOR THERMAL TRANSFER PRINTERS Thermal transfer printers such as the QMS ColorScript series provide a quick and easy way to transfer a color image from computer screen to paper (10). To put color on the page, these printers use thermally sensitive color sheeting in the process colors—cyan, magenta, yellow and sometimes black. The printer *rasterizes* a digital image from a graphics file (that is, it turns the graphics instructions into a dot pattern specific for that printer). To print each of the four colors, the dot pattern for this color is applied to the page by heat and pressure from the pins in a printhead that fuses dots of color to the page. As the color sheet moves past the printhead, each pin in the printhead is either heated (to put a dot on the page) or not heated (to leave that dot space blank). The page makes three or four passes through the printer, with one color applied on each pass, resulting in a four-color print. A full range of colors is produced when the tiny dots of the process colors, all the same size, are mixed on the page in dithered patterns (see "Dithering" in Chapter 2).

CONTINUOUS-TONE PRINTERS Dye sublimation printers, such as the Kodak XLS 8600 and XLS 8600PS (11), also use heat to apply color to the page. In this case, although the printers produce a relatively low number of dots per inch, the color

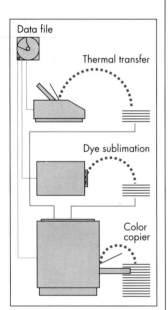

9 Short-run composite color printing can be accomplished by going directly from an image file stored on disk to a thermal transfer printer, a dye sublimation printer or a color copier. When high-quality color is not required, a thermal transfer or dye-sublimation print, or a continuous-tone print, can be used as an original from which color copies are made.

Choosing a Printing Process

With film-based printing processes the major costs of printing a page are in preparing film, making a color proof, making the printing plates from the film and putting plates and ink on the press. Once that's done, the cost per page of putting ink on paper is very low.

In color printing by thermal transfer, dye sublimation or xerography, on the other hand, the "up-front" costs of getting the machine configured to print are much less. A much larger proportion of the cost is in the materials — the color transfer sheets, color ribbons or toner cartridges and in some cases special paper and processing chemicals. Assuming that all of the processes produce acceptable color for a particular project, which process is most economical depends on how many pages you need to print. For small editions and especially for publications that change often—such as menus, programs or covers for membership directories—nonpress composite color processes can make sense.

10 Like other thermal transfer printers, the QMS ColorScript series of printers prints images from disk, using four transfer sheets of color—cyan, magenta, yellow and black. Mixed colors are produced by a dithering process that serves well for producing color comps. This color patterning can also be incorporated as an integral part of the texture of an image. This FreeHand drawing was output on a QMS ColorScript printer.

11 The Kodak XLS 8600 and XLS 8600PS printers produce images that looks like continuous-tone color photos. In these and other dye sublimation printers, colors are mixed by varying dot size, which is accomplished by regulating the amount of heat applied at each point in the image. Because the colors are not dithered, the dot pattern is not obvious.

print looks like the continuous-tone of a photograph. That's because the pins in the printhead can be heated to many different temperatures. The degree of heat applied to the pin determines how much of the dye or ink from a color transfer ribbon is applied to the dot. By controlling the amount of dye released, dye sublimation printers can mix colors without dithering to produce a continuous-tone image. Other continuous-tone printers, such as the Iris inkjet and 3M's Rainbow, are too sophisticated and expensive for desktop use, but prints from these machines are available from many imagesetting service bureaus. Their output looks very much like pages printed from separated film at high screen resolutions. They're useful for short print runs, for which it's too expensive to produce film and pay press setup charges, and for documents that are too large to produce with desktop color printers. They can also provide a kind of digital proofing before you go to the expense of making film separations.

OUTPUT TO COLOR COPIERS Because thermal transfer and dye sublimation prints cost more per copy than pages produced on color photocopiers such as the Canon Color Laser Copier (CLC) series or the Kodak ColorEdge, one way to print short-run color is to produce an "original" with a thermal transfer or dye sublimation printer and then use a color copier to reproduce it in quantity. Color copiers work by thermal transfer, photographic or xerographic processes. The xerographic process uses a laser to set up a dot pattern on a printing drum, and toner is bound or repelled according to the charge at each dot location. Heat is then used to fuse the toner to the paper.

As desktop color has developed into a major force in publishing and printing, color copiers have been adapted to receive the information for printing from a digital file. For example, the Canon CLC and Kodak ColorEdge copiers can accept graphics files stored on disk (12).

POSTSCRIPT OR NOT? Desktop color printers that incorporate the PostScript language can rasterize (that is, translate) the object-oriented artwork and halftone screens from a PostScript-based graphics file into the dot patterns needed to print the page. To build PostScript into their machines, however, manufacturers must pay a fee to Adobe Systems, Inc., the developers of PostScript. For a low-cost color printer, this fee can be a substantial part of the price. So to keep costs down, some desktop color printers are produced without PostScript. A printer that isn't equipped with PostScript can still print PostScript files if it includes a *PostScript clone*, an interpreter that mimics the rasterization done by PostScript. Another alternative is special software that rasterizes PostScript files for non-PostScript printers.

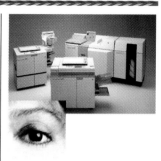

12 The Kodak ColorEdge copier can produce images like this one directly from disk at 300 dots per inch. The color reproduction produced by color copiers is quite suitable for many short-run color printing applications.

A COLOR-MANAGEMENT SYSTEM is used to make color as consistent as possible from one desktop publishing device to another. In systems such as those of EFI and Kodak, each input, display or output device is characterized in terms of its color *gamut*, or the range of colors it can reproduce. Through a set of tables of color data for these devices, the system "knows" what kinds of color characteristics to expect from each device and how to translate between them. For instance, it can analyze the color data gathered by a scanner, predict how a particular imagesetter will output that data, and figure out how to accurately preview the image on a particular model of monitor.

Although color management programs, current system software and the second generation of the PostScript page-description language all include developments to help keep color consistent, all are limited in their effectiveness. A more reliable way to get predictable color is to do a kind of back-to-front color matching, adjusting the screen display of an electronic file to match the output generated from that file on a particular printer, so that artwork later designed with the same monitor settings and printed with the same printer will produce predictable results.

BACK-TO-FRONT COLOR MATCHING With or without a color management system, back-to-front color matching is probably the most reliable way to get predictable color. Here's one way to do it: Early in the project, design a piece of artwork according to the color you see on your monitor screen. Then produce the file all the way to film separations and proof print, or, better yet, to a press proof. Go back and adjust the monitor settings so the color in the file as displayed on-screen looks like the print. Now any additional image-editing changes you make to the artwork on-screen should carry through when you print from the file.

Ideally, using this back-to-front color-matching process is the best way to account for the results of all the color changes that occur throughout the entire prepress and on-press processes, including the characteristics of individual monitors and output devices, RGB-to-CMYK conversion and dot gain. In reality, this kind of color matching can be very expensive as it requires taking artwork all the way to proof or print.

Instead of a special press test, the artwork can sometimes be "tagged on" to another job that goes through the same prepress and printing process. Or a similar project can be used for color matching. For instance, if you're designing the third in a series of brochures, you can take one of the first two publications, open its electronic file, and without changing the file itself, adjust the monitor's color until, to your eye, the screen

13 By varying the settings used for output on the imagesetter, a service bureau can get a range of color proofs from the same digital image file. Then, by comparing the file as shown on the monitor with the range of prints, the artist chooses the print that looks most like the display. The service bureau can then use the settings that produced this print when outputting files from that artist's desktop system.

display matches the print. Then any further artwork you design with these monitor settings and run through the same prepress and printing processes (including the settings used for imagesetting) should produce results that look like the display.

Still another way to match color is to have a service bureau produce several versions of a color file, using (and noting) various imagesetter settings, and then compile a set of proof prints from all versions of the image. With this print and an electronic version of the artwork on disk, you can open the electronic file on-screen, choose the printed version that best matches it,

14 The Radius PrecisionColor Calibrator attaches to a color display and evaluates and then corrects variations in the color display that can occur over time. Calibrating the monitor is an essential part of overall system color matching.

and notify the service bureau which one you've chosen. Service bureau personnel can then use the imagesetter settings for that version whenever they receive a file from your system (13).

CALIBRATING THE PARTS OF THE SYSTEM Whether you use a color management system or a back-to-front matching process, you need to be sure that each individual part of the design and prepress system gives repeatable results—that, given the same electronic data on two separate days, the display screen will display the same colors.

Calibrators are available to ensure that monitors continue to meet the factory standards for display, so that they present the same color day after day (14). Many designers find that calibrating monitors weekly ensures predictable performance. Another factor in keeping on-screen color constant is the monitor's environment. To minimize the effect of color reflections and variation in ambient lighting, you can shade the windows to minimize the effect of the changing daylight and keep the room lighting constant, paint the walls a neutral color and even be careful not to wear bright clothing.

Still another factor in matching color is the artist's eye. Human color perception varies greatly. Both the color management system and back-to-front color matching can take this into account, with the artist comparing the on-screen version with the proof or the printed piece.

At the output end of the prepress process, the service bureau that does the imagesetting must also keep its equipment calibrated. That means controlling the type of paper or film used, adjusting the intensity of the laser that images the dots on the film, and routinely changing the developer in the film processor. All will affect the color produced by the halftone dot patterns on the film. To get predictable results, an imagesetting service bureau needs to consistently use high-quality film, to adjust the imagesetter's laser settings for changes in film and changes in resolution, and to change the processing chemicals before they get weak enough so that putting in fresh solutions causes a marked change in the look of processed film. A calibration system such as Kodak's Precision Imagesetter Linearization Software creates customized calibration sets for different kinds of film, in order to keep the laser settings adjusted to produce accurate and predictable results.

FOR MANY DESKTOP COLOR PROJECTS the imagesetting service bureau is the essential link between the artist or designer and the printer. After you've produced digital files that achieve your design and color objectives and you've checked with the printer to find out what kind of film separations are required, it's up to the service bureau to produce that film from your files. For that process to go smoothly—producing the right result and meeting the printing deadline—you need to choose an appropriate service bureau for the job and supply its imagesetting professionals with the files and information they need. Typically, the service bureau carries out the following steps:

• Receives the files you've produced with your illustration or page layout program.

• Copies the files from your transport medium (such as SyQuest cartridges) to the bureau's own storage system. (This step ensures that if something happens to the files during processing, your originals will be intact. Although you should always make your own backup copy before you send the files out, this extra backup adds security.)

• Generates the PostScript files necessary for separation, in the process checking to see that all associated art files are present. (Instead of supplying application files as described above, you can supply the PostScript files yourself. The advantage is that you leave no opportunity for the service bureau to introduce errors into your files at this step; the disadvantage is that it takes time and effort, and the responsibility for error is entirely yours.)

• Produces the film separations.

• Makes proofs (usually composite proofs such as Matchprints) from that film.

• Delivers the film and proofs to you or the printer, also returning your original files on your transport media.

• Invoices you for the job.

Departures from these procedures may include electronic transfer rather than physical delivery of files; digital proofing (producing a color print directly from the file so you can review it before committing to the expense of making film); or producing printing plates directly from the file, eliminating the film step.

CHOOSING A SERVICE BUREAU Three factors that designers look for in a service bureau's performance are high quality, speed and low cost. Also of great value is the willingness to help solve the problems that almost inevitably arise in a large or complex job. Here are some tips for choosing the right service bureau to do the job:

• It's important to develop a good, consistent working relationship with a service bureau you can depend on, but sometimes you may want to use more than one provider. One service bureau may be the least expensive, the quickest and excellent for black-and-white output, but not great at producing color separations. Another may produce outstanding color separations but may not be able to turn jobs around quickly.

• Do some comparison shopping. Most service bureaus update their equipment and training continuously. Even if you have one or two companies that you work with regularly, it's a good idea to compare costs and capabilities once in while. You can prepare a description of the job (see "What the Service Bureau Needs to Know" on page 70) and fax it to several companies for bids. In evaluating bids, it pays to investigate those that are much higher or lower than most of the others: A low bidder may not fully understand what you need; a high bidder may be planning to provide more service than you require. In addition to the bid itself, the response time and kinds of questions each service bureau asks in costing the job can provide you with insights about their competence. The hoped-for outcome of the bidding process is that you can confidently go with the lowest bidder. But keep in mind that the lowest bid is not always the most economical in the end. Mistakes, even if the service bureau reruns your pages "at no cost" will delay your job.

• Make sure the service bureau you choose can handle the kinds of files you produce. Some service bureaus are reluctant to handle files from certain drawing or page layout applications—even some of the major programs. Unless you're willing to buy and use the program that a particular service bureau prefers, you need to find a provider that will run the files you like to produce. To run your files effectively, the service bureau must have technical support from the appropriate software companies; this becomes especially important when new versions of the software are released. Most of the major desktop publishing software companies provide some technical training or other support for imagesetter operators and maintain lists of "authorized" service bureaus. You can check with these companies for their listings, and also ask the service bureaus how they keep up-to-date on the programs you use.

• Look at quality control. Keeping equipment calibrated and chemicals replenished is essential for producing film separation and color proofs that are consistent over time. Ask about calibration procedures and schedules and how often film density is checked. Many good service bureaus check daily to see that their imagesetters are producing the halftone dot densities called for by their calibration standards.

• Look at the work flow. Almost as important as technical quality control is adequate work flow management. For example, if the service bureau is not efficient about transferring film from imagesetter operators to proofing technicians, your job can sit in limbo until you call to check on it. This costs you not only the time already lost but additional time while you wait for someone to track it down and put it back in the work stream. Another problem that can delay your job is a lack of sufficient supplies and materials because reordering procedures aren't up to par.

WHAT THE SERVICE BUREAU NEEDS TO KNOW Once you've narrowed down your choice of service bureaus, it's a good idea, especially for a large or complex job, to sit down with a representative and discuss how the output will proceed. The bureau will need to know when the job will be ready to start and how quickly you will provide additional files. The service bureau may be able to suggest scheduling or proofing options that will expedite the job or reduce costs.

If you'll be sending page layout files, you should review the file formats you intend to use for supplying the linked artwork files (see "Graphics File Formats" on page 19). QuarkXPress and PageMaker, for example, may require different file formats. And supplying TIFF files in CMYK rather than RGB format may eliminate a step in separating the page layout file, saving time and money.

Find out what sort of low-resolution proofs you should provide along with your files and how much responsibility the service bureau will take for checking the film output against the prints you supply. For example, will a technician check the film output against a composite laser proof to make sure all artwork has been imaged and all typefaces are correct before making a Matchprint from the film? Both you and the bureau should understand how much checking the bureau will do at each step in the output process and who will accept the responsibility if film or proofs need to be redone.

Find out whether the service bureau charges by the minute for files that take a long time to output. Set a cutoff time after which the imagesetter technician should stop the run and call you for instructions if a file is taking extraordinarily long.

When you're ready to send files for output, the service bureau will require certain information. Many service bureaus have their own submission forms that request the information they need. With or without a form, here are some things they'll want to know:

• File name: What files to output

• Program of origin: What software was used to produce the file

• Page numbers: Which pages of a multiple-page document to output

• Percent reduction or enlargement: Whether to output at the designed size (100%) or at some other size

• Page size: Which of several standard-size pages of film output you would like; for example, 8.5 x 11, 10 x 12, or 11.5 x 17 inches (Some service bureaus charge for film output by the linear inch instead of using standard page sizes; this can save you money on small or odd-size documents.)

• Marks: Whether you want the imagesetter to add crop marks (to delineate the edges of the pages) or registration marks (to align the negatives for proofing or printing)

• Separations: Whether to output as color separations (CMYK or custom color) or as composites (without separating the colors) (If color separations are requested, the bureau will need to know whether all color plates are to be output, or only certain ones.)

• Positive or negative: Which type of film output your printer requires

• Emulsion: Whether you want the film to read correctly with the emulsion side down or with the emulsion side up (Many printers in the United States require film that is negative and right-reading when the emulsion side is down, but printers elsewhere in the world may have different requirements.)

• Line screen: What halftone screen resolution is to be used for output

• Proofs: What kind of proofing is required for each page (Making laminate proofs such as Matchprints from film positives rather than negatives requires different proofing material than proofing from negatives and is also a more difficult process; not all service bureaus that make film separations and proofs are able to provide proof from positive film.)

• Additional services: Whether you'll need the service bureau to do additional work on your files, such as trapping (see page 42) or imposition of pages into the large layouts the printer will use to print a multipage publication (in which case the service bureau will need instructions from the printer)

• Other: Whether you want your files to be given other than the standard treatment (What the service bureau considers to be standard may depend more on the default settings of the separation software the bureau uses than on what designers or printers typically require; for example, even though most page layouts are designed to be separated so that black type overprints background colors, some separation software has to be specifically set to overprint black ink.)

• Date due: When you need the job to be finished (You can expect to pay extra—even double or triple—if you need service much faster than normal turnaround time.)

• Contact: Who to call (and at what telephone number during what hours) if a problem develops

For any complex job, unforeseen problems can arise, due to bugs in the software, incompatibility of file types, and so on. You will probably have to absorb the cost of fixing and rerunning the files in these cases, but the service bureau's willingness to help you figure out what's wrong and solve the problem can be a welcome kind of support.

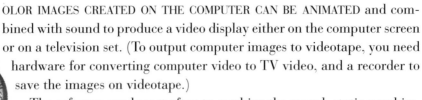

COLOR IMAGES CREATED ON THE COMPUTER CAN BE ANIMATED and combined with sound to produce a video display either on the computer screen or on a television set. (To output computer images to videotape, you need hardware for converting computer video to TV video, and a recorder to save the images on videotape.)

The software used most often to combine the sound, static graphics, video, animation and type that make up multimedia consists of authoring programs such as Macromedia's Director and Authorware Professional, Asymetrix's Multimedia Toolkit and Passport's Producer.

Interactive multimedia takes the mix of media a step further, allowing the viewer to become a participant in the on-screen presentation. An interface to the multimedia presentation is designed to invite the viewer to respond to the screen display, making choices or entering data that affect the way the presentation proceeds.

Many of the design and color considerations are the same in multimedia as they are for print. But on-screen display does present its own kinds of color challenges for the designer.

DESIGNING INTERACTIVE INTERFACES To make it easy for people inexperienced with multimedia to recognize the active areas of the screen that can be touched or clicked with a cursor, you can design an interface that includes graphic representations of buttons (15). As interactive multimedia becomes more commonplace and its users more experienced, the need for the button metaphor becomes less critical, and standard typeset labels familiar from print design can be used to designate the active areas (16).

DESIGNING FOR THE LOWEST COMMON DENOMINATOR Designed for on-screen display, multimedia interfaces use the RGB color gamut. But while multimedia authors often use full-color 24-bit systems, the people who buy and use the multimedia products may have systems with a smaller color range—16-bit or 8-bit systems. So it's best to design with the audience's machines in mind. For example, using the Apple System palette to assign colors to the on-screen graphics for

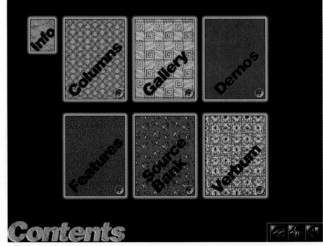

15 The "Contents" screen from Verbum Interactive 1.0, a multimedia magazine that runs on the desktop, includes realistic looking pushbuttons. The buttons, designed in Adobe Illustrator and then converted to pixel-based graphics in Adobe Photoshop, provide a familiar way for readers to interact with this on-screen magazine.

multimedia that will run on Macintosh computers will ensure that colors appear bright and uniform, not dithered. (Dithering is mixing dots of several colors to make up an intermediate color; for more about dithering, see page 13.) Assembling your own patterns made with System colors lets you control the color mix.

USING TYPE ON-SCREEN Type can be difficult to read on-screen, but following some simple design rules can help make both text and display type effective.

• You can get a variety of good-looking typefaces on-screen by using PostScript fonts along with Adobe Type Manager (ATM) to provide smooth character outlines.

• Use sans serif or simple serif typefaces. When displayed at the low resolution of the desktop computer screen (often 72 dpi), typefaces with strokes of uniform thickness make more readable text than the thick-and-thin strokes or ornate curls of more decorative typefaces.

• In general, keep on-screen text to a minimum. Pop-out text blocks that appear and expand only when the viewer makes a selection on-screen, or text that scrolls within a text box of limited size, makes written information easily available without cluttering the interface with a daunting amount of type.

• Set text in relatively large type (no smaller than 10 points), and set columns relatively narrow. Trying to follow long lines of text across an entire screen can be hard work.

• Choose text and background colors for readability. Black text on a pale background is familiar and relatively readable, compared to white or colored text or black text on a brightly colored background.

"CAPTURING" POSTSCRIPT GRAPHICS The graphics produced for display by multimedia authoring programs are pixel-based, not PostScript-based. That's because desktop computer systems, by and large, haven't been designed to directly convert the mathematical formulas of PostScript to a screen display. But you can still get the advantages of object-oriented drawing and page layout in designing for multimedia. Design the graphics or layouts with your favorite PostScript-based program, using all the drawing, typesetting and layout features you like. Use Adobe Type Manager to get the best possible screen display for type and adjust the PostScript program's Preferences settings to give you high-resolution graphics display. Then use a screen-capturing program (software that captures the information sent to the monitor and records it as a pixel-based image file) to convert the artwork or layout to a pixel-based format that your authoring software can use. Within the authoring program, or with image-editing software, you can crop or refine the screen capture or combine it with other graphics to complete a screen.

16 The graphic interface for this interactive point-of-purchase display for beard shampoo was designed without obvious buttons.

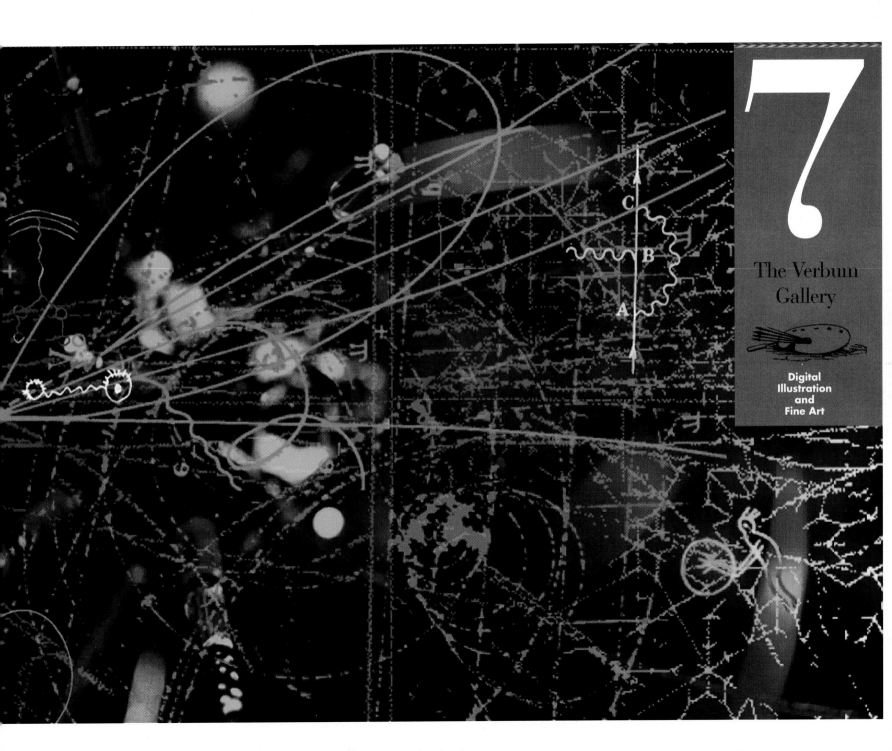

7

The Verbum
Gallery

**Digital
Illustration
and
Fine Art**

Opening Spread:
Detail from "Dome" by
Jeff Brice, page 90.

THE FOLLOWING PAGES showcase illustrative works by top artists working with state-of-the-art digital tools. Use this gallery as a source of ideas and inspiration—or simply enjoy it as a fine art experience. Although we chose these works primarily for their artistic content, they are in fact the result of technically competent use of the tools, and the artists have provided some helpful information about how the works were developed.

You may notice here a large proportion of montage, or "blendo," work combining photographic and illustrative imagery in unusual ways. We have seen this kind of art evolve for 10 years now as artists have experimented with the wide range of programs available, exploring their interoperability. Certainly, clean PostScript illustration with programs such as FreeHand and Adobe Illustrator predominate in technical and commercial illustration (many of the illus-

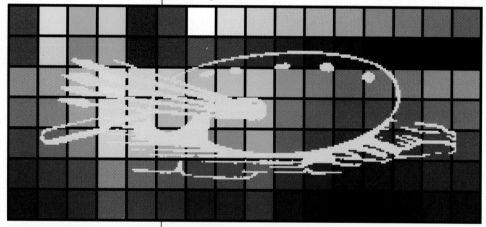

trations throughout the first six chapters of *The Desktop Color Book* are PostScript works), but the use of the painterly and special-effects capabilities of Adobe Photoshop and Fractal Design Painter, combined with scanned imagery and even 3D rendering, is more and more evident among those illus-

trators who are pioneering innovations in style and technique.

THE GALLERY TRADITION This Gallery represents the latest in a series of Verbum Galleries. In the early days of desktop publishing, *Verbum* magazine featured the highly regarded Gallery section, the first showcase for artists working in the digital realm. Later, the many Verbum books included Gallery sections. We also assembled the "Imagine" exhibits of Personal Computer Art, which were shown in San Diego, San Francisco, Boston, Tokyo and other cities. *Verbum Interactive*, the first CD-ROM magazine, published in the fall of 1991, was the venue for the first interactive multimedia and computer animation Gallery. Finally, the Verbum Gallery existed as a physical art space in downtown San Diego, functioning for two years as one of the first dedicated digital fine art galleries in the country. We are pleased to offer this latest version of the Verbum Gallery in *The Desktop Color Book*. We hope you enjoy it!

Dominique de Bardonneche-Berglund

Adobe Photoshop

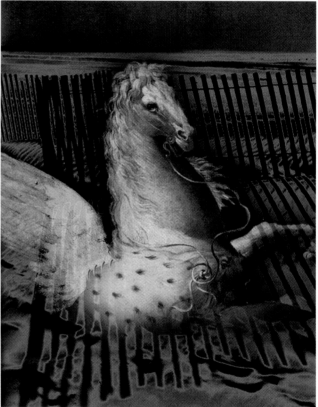

Le Grand Récit (left) represents vertigo: "Come," says the abyss, "I am nothing." It began with a selection from a personal database of backgrounds, one with many nearly invisible cracks, opened in Photoshop. Onto the background, through a mask with a left-to-right gradation, was pasted a moonlit landscape. Part of a portrait by Hans Memling was scanned and pasted in with composite controls, and the silhouette of the man was added at 50% transparency.

The most difficult aspect of creating **Pégase Prisonnier** (above) was to seamlessly attach the wings (from a scanned Baroque painting of an angel) to the horse (cut out from a scan of a 17th-century equestrian painting). Photoshop's feathering function was used here as well as in selecting the horse to make the legs partially transparent when pasted over a background created by compositing two overlapping images with the Difference command.

Noces à la Nuit (near right) is a "fusion" of three images in Photoshop. Scanned images of the golden frescoes of Pompeii and a sand dune were composited. Then a detail from a painting by Piero Della Francesca was scanned and the face was selected with a highly feathered lasso, copied and pasted into the composite. While the pasted selection was still floating, the lasso was used with the Command key to subtract parts of the left edge of the face to fuse it with the dune-hair.

Les Voyages Perdus (right) represents nostalgia for unrealized possibilities. A scan of a detail from a painting—buildings lining a street—was pasted into a black background in Photoshop. A scan of a second painting was pasted onto the first in the Multiply mode. Then the first painting was added again, this time flipped to face the opposite direction. The small people in the foreground are a detail from a painting by Jan Bruegel the Elder. Each of the frames was pasted into the composition, and parts were removed with the lasso and Command key before the pasted selection was released to become part of the image.

Adventures in the Life of a Fairy, Scene V is part of a series of "fairy" images that combine the innocence of youth with the foreshadowing of a fateful future.

Five separate photographs were scanned. In addition, the fairy's wings, which are eucalyptus leaves, the birth control pills and the dispenser were all objects placed directly onto the flatbed scanner. In Photoshop colors were changed and transparencies were adjusted before these elements were combined.

The Add Noise filter was applied to the fairy's "suit" to produce the sparkle effect. The Defringe filter and composite controls were used on the cross behind her.

➤ The Blur or Blur More filter can be useful for creating smooth transitions in blending images together.

Madonna on the Edge is an abstract photo-illustration that combines elements from several different images. Five separate photographs were scanned at 180 dpi.

The color and transparency were manipulated in Photoshop to heighten the color and to create an ethereal atmosphere.

The background is a scanned photo of a crater on the island of Maui. Colors were altered and the Find Edges filter was applied to the image. The Gaussian Blur filter was also applied at various settings. Shadows were painted in to anchor the figure on the rock.

➤ You can create a relatively natural-looking group of figures (like the flamingos here) by copying and pasting an identical image several times, flipping some of the pasted elements horizontally, scaling them and otherwise adjusting and moving them to give the repetition a less uniform pattern.

**Under the Big Top,
Side Show II** is one in a five-part
series of photo-illustrations whose
subject is the carnival sideshow in
several unusual and imaginative
incarnations.

Thirteen different photographs
were scanned and composited
in Photoshop. Hair was added to
the Madonnas, crucifixes and a
flower were placed in their hands,
makeup was "applied," and
shadows were drawn in to give
the final image a realistic look.

An individual handbill (seen in
the lower left corner of this image)
was developed for each of the
five compositions in this series.
The handbill was pasted into a
scanned frame, the Perspective
effect was applied to tilt the frame
slightly, and shadows were drawn
in to help integrate this addition
into the image.

Adobe Photoshop,
ColorStudio,
Specular Collage

Columbus Legacy, a photo montage, was begun in ColorStudio. A woodcut of Columbus's ships landing on America's shores was scanned and used to make a grayscale mask. The same process was used with the image of the woman. The contrast of both grayscale masks was increased by using the Freehand option in the Color Correction palette. Mask Options was used to combine parts of the two images.

➤ When merging two or more images, be sure to save the resized versions so you can work back and forth between the originals and the combined piece to strengthen the details you want to keep and obliterate the extraneous detail.

Behind the Veil was created in Photoshop from scanned and manipulated imagery. A page scanned from the Koran was made high-contrast by adjusting Curves, and the colors were inverted, turning it into a negative. To make it appear to be floating in front of the image of the young woman, the blank space of the page was dropped out as the image was pasted over the face in Lighten mode.

➤ Unique prints can be made not only from Iris editioning but also by using a Polaroid transfer process: A Xerox 770 print can be rephotographed and the two parts of the instant film can be separated. With an application of developing gel, the image can then be placed face down on a damp sheet of watercolor paper of corresponding size to make a transfer. A soft focus and rough edges created by the instant film transfer are identifying marks of this process.

Map of the Future is a montage of scanned photographs created in Photoshop. The photo of the child was first pasted onto the image of the astrological chart, dropping away the skin tones to create a high-contrast image. Parts of the chart were then brought back into some of the light areas of the image by cloning from the previously saved chart image.

The contrast was intensified using the Levels controls, and the colors of the star, circle and square were enhanced by adjusting hue and saturation.

Adobe Photoshop

Myth and Mystery (far right) and **Travel by Land** (right) were both part of a banner installation at the Inverness Rail Station in Inverness, Scotland. They were created in 1993 as a commission from Fotofeis, the Scottish international festival of photography. The banners were silkscreened on 44 x 26-foot pieces of fabric.

The project began with extensive research on the culture of the Scottish Highlands. Photographs, illustrations, slides and stories were gathered as source materials for the images. Many of these materials, including the text elements, were scanned into Photoshop. The bilingual approach was very important from both design and cultural perspectives, both languages (Gaelic and English) having played a critical role in forming and maintaining the Scottish Highlands culture.

➤ Collecting a library of scanned imagery on storage disks so that you have easy access to a broad range of images can facilitate the process of creating a montage.

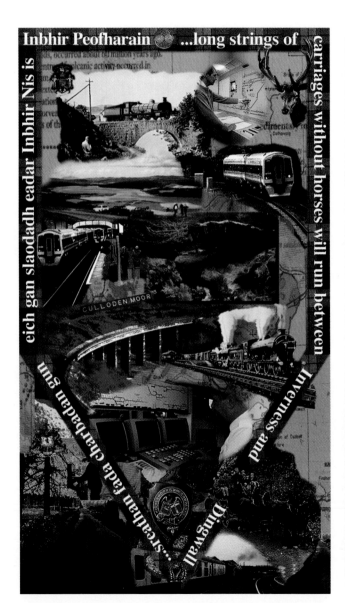

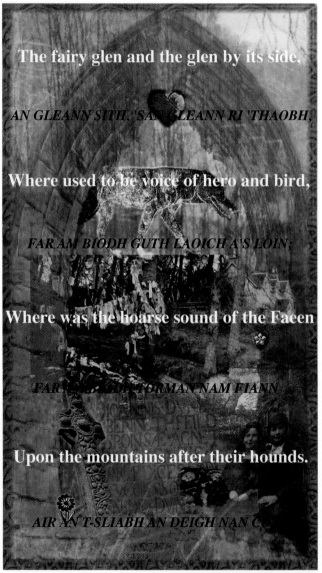

The fairy glen and the glen by its side,

AN GLEANN SITH, 'SAN GLEANN RI 'THAOBH,

Where used to be voice of hero and bird,

FAR AM BIODH GUTH LAOICH A'S LOIN;

Where was the hoarse sound of the Faeen

FAR AM BIODH TORMAN NAM FIANN

Upon the mountains after their hounds.

AIR AN T-SLIABH AN DEIGH NAN CO

Adobe Photoshop

Escalation (above), **Stardust** (upper right) and **Spiral Nebulae** (lower right) are concerned with the artificial landscapes of industrial enclaves, highways and commercial strips. Referencing the surreal urban landscape of Las Vegas, this work explores a mysterious and distorted world of exaggerated and unnatural color, reflected light and fragments of illuminated signage.

The layered composited imagery evokes the passage of time and the continuing cycle of urban disintegration and regeneration. The images express the hidden dynamism of the urban and industrial landscape, which appear to have a life of their own, without a discernible human presence. An artificial, exaggerated color spectrum accentuates a sense of desolation. The seductive and engaging city lights indicate a troubling separation from nature, human identity and community.

Adobe Photoshop,
PhotoStyler

Both **Running on Faith** (right) and **Calling All Angels** (above) were produced as limited-edition Iris prints. Each is a montage of as many as 50 separate snapshots, scanned into PhotoStyler. Color and value were corrected and a mask was made for each component.

The natural, reflective quality of the water was created by compositing the sky and trees with the other elements and by using drawing and painting tools to create texture. A photo of Christmas tree lights added "sparks" and surface tension. The edges of the montaged photos were seamed together with the blend and duplication tools. Some edges were left pixelated to reference the digital medium.

Adobe Photoshop

Bee Priestesses 1A and **Glucose Goddess II** were produced as part of a large installation entitled *Dance of the Melissae*, which focuses on the honeybee society as a metaphor of nature and its relationship to science and technology. They were two of 100 components that formed the *Honeycomb Wall*. Both were output as 11.5 x 11.5-inch Cibachrome prints mounted on hexagonal wooden panels.

Bee Priestesses 1A began with a scanned slide of a candle against a lead background, placed on the hexagonal template created in Photoshop. A second scan of a black-and-white image of beehives was pasted into the first scan at 65% opacity. The third scan, of a woman wearing a beekeeper's hat, was flipped horizontally and placed onto the first scan using Photoshop's Luminosity mode and a transparency of about 50%. The rubber stamp tool was used to clean up areas where uneven transitions resulted from the overlying scans. A close-up of a bee and a second version of the wings alone were pasted last; the Hue and Saturation modes were used to achieve a luminous and translucent effect.

➤ Photoshop's transparency controls and compositing modes are worth exploring. They can be used to create delicate and evocative layered images.

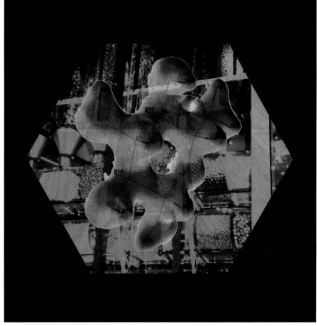

For **Glucose Goddess II** a slide of a candy factory was pasted onto the hexagonal template using the Luminosity mode in the composite controls of Photoshop. A scanned slide of a molecule of glucose, previously created using chemical modeling software on an SGI workstation and photographed from the screen, was then placed over the image of the candy factory. After the colors were inverted, the image was pasted in the Luminosity mode at a 35% opacity to create a more dimensional effect.

Fractal Design Painter

Earth Dream was created in Painter by compositing four different original photographs taken by the artist. Liquid Media, Glass Distortion and a variable location cloner were used to blend the photographs.

Untitled/Trees was made by compositing four photos in Painter, using a soft cloner and a variable location cloner. One of the photos had been converted from a color scan to grayscale using Color Overlay. Liquid Media was then used to distort this image before it was composited with the rest of the photos.

Adobe Photoshop,
Specular Collage,
Gallery Effects,
Kai's Power Tools,
Fractal Design Painter,
FreeHand,
ColorStudio

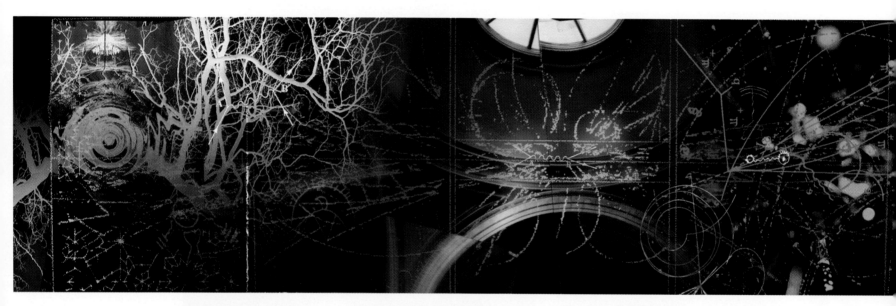

Dome was created as a promotional bookmark. Several images were scanned on a flatbed scanner; other scans were obtained with Photo CD processing. All the scans were imported into Photoshop as RGB files.

Each image was retouched and a selection boundary was created and stored in a fourth channel. The extra channel acted like a mask in Collage, where these images were composited. The mask for the dome photo included a right-to-left gradient so the image would fade when composited.

The image of the particle tracks was made to glow using the Gallery Effects Diffuse Glow filter. The glowing particle tracks were then pasted into an alpha channel to be used as a mask. This mask was loaded into the RGB channel of the composite image, and the KPT Gradient Designer was used to create a spectrum within the tracks.

Scans were composited, resized and overlaid using various masks and composite techniques. The final image was rendered at 300 dpi.

Idea was created for the cover of a brochure designed for IDEA by Richard Hamilton of Grafik Communications, Ltd. The photos were scanned on a flatbed scanner and a background texture was created in Painter X2, using Watercolor Pastel on a Heavy paper texture. The star grid was created in FreeHand.

The photos and background were then opened in ColorStudio, and the Color Curves were used to adjust the color, making the circuitry gold. The FreeHand star chart was imported into the Shapes annex and rasterized.

All of the elements were composited onto the background using the mask layers. The star chart was first. Then the lines were composited, along with a graduated fill from black to light blue. The clouds were composited with a transparency. The water was faded into the image so that the background could show through. After the circuit grid, the hand and the line drawing were added last.

Mike Swartzbeck

Adobe Photoshop

Sky Gate3, the third in a series of explorations of the concept of flight, windows and passage, is a Photoshop montage of original photos of the local neighborhood and the French Quarter of New Orleans. The jangling, out-of-register RGB effect laid over the bricks was created by scanning a photo of ivy on a wall, moving it slightly on the scanner glass as the lamp made repeated passes beneath it to produce the RGB image, and then combining it with the bricks using the Calculate effects Add and Blend. The image of the wall with the barred window was modified with the Distort effect; the "ghostly" or "spiritual" effect of light passing through the bars was created by copying a portion of the wall/window image and treating it with the Facet, Gaussian Blur and Find Edges filters.

Urban Light3 is a Photoshop montage from original photos and found objects. Photos of newly blooming dogwoods, a building under construction and a daffodil plucked from the front yard and pressed in the scanner were combined to form an abstraction that suggests a low-flying aerial view of a city at night. The dogwood photo was solarized and treated with repeated applications of the Gaussian Blur, Facet and Find Edges filters. The building photo was converted to grayscale and used as a mask for dropping in the dogwood image. The scanned daffodil was treated with the Mosaic and Find Edges filters before being laid over the background with two Calculate functions, Lighter and Add.

➤ When you get so comfortable with a certain repertoire of effects that you're using them without thinking about it, it may be a good time to put aside an evening or two to do nothing but experiment with effects you haven't tried yet, without worrying if you don't come out with a usable piece of work at the end.

Mom's Shocking Encounter is a Photoshop montage of found images. It consists almost entirely of fragments from a favorite issue of a weekly tabloid newspaper, featuring one of their standard space alien abduction stories. The pages were scanned in grayscale, then converted to RGB and treated with color in Photoshop. They were combined with photos of organ pipes that had been treated with the Facet and Find Edges filters and the Distort function. The newspaper images were added with the Calculate Blend and Add effects. The "tangled thread" and halo-like effect seen throughout were done with the Find Edges filter and the Darker and Add Calculate effects.

Adobe Photoshop,
Fractal Design Painter,
Kai's Power Tools, Xaos Tools,
Infini-D, Studio 8

Verbum Batik is a Photoshop painting that includes both text and scanned imagery. The fractal patterns were created with the KPT Fractal Explorer. The type was set in an alpha channel and loaded into the RGB channel as a selection, and various filters were applied.

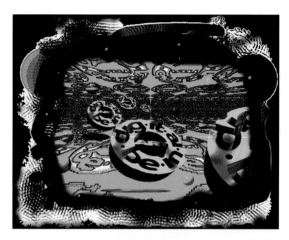

BE-INvironment was created as a promotional illustration for Verbum's sixth annual Digital Art Be-In. The floating Be-In logos were modeled in Infini-D. The abstract space into which they were placed was created using mapped perspectives in Studio 8. The three-dimensional look of the floating spheres was created in Photoshop with filters from Kai's Power Tools. These elements were assembled in Photoshop, and the border was added in Painter.

Fractoid represents "the digital yin/yang." It was generated in Photoshop from algorithms set up with Kai's Power Tools. The image was further developed and detailed in Painter.

Goz Zoom was designed as an interactive environment that the viewer can "fly into" on the computer to explore the image of Michael Gosney placed deep in his digital forest. The portrait photo was scanned in and manipulated in Photoshop. Outlying textures and objects were drawn in Photoshop and composited.

The detail of the image increases as the viewer zooms in on certain areas, exploring the piece as a kind of landscape or architecture. This possibility was created by working on the image in an enlarged format to develop a very tightly composed, finished surface that would stand up to magnification.

Adobe Photoshop

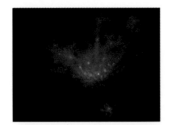

Both **Emission Nebula** (top) and **Black Hole** (bottom) were done in Photoshop for the Oregon Museum of Science and Industry's *Star Trek: Federation Science* touring exhibit. Both graphics appeared in the navigator's console on the bridge of the Enterprise starship.

For **Emission Nebula** the basic starfield was created with a single-pixel airbrush in Photoshop. Washes of color were roughed in with a wide airbrush at a low Opacity setting. The smudge tool was used to feather and shape the cloud. Glows within the cloud were airbrushed in, and then stars were overlaid on the glows.

For **Black Hole** Photoshop's pen tool was used to define the shape of both the red star and the diagonal beam. Each of these outlines was turned into a selection and filled with a gradient. The smudge tool, operated via a Wacom tablet, was used to pull color off the surface of the star and blend it into the disk at the right. Image details were airbrushed in.

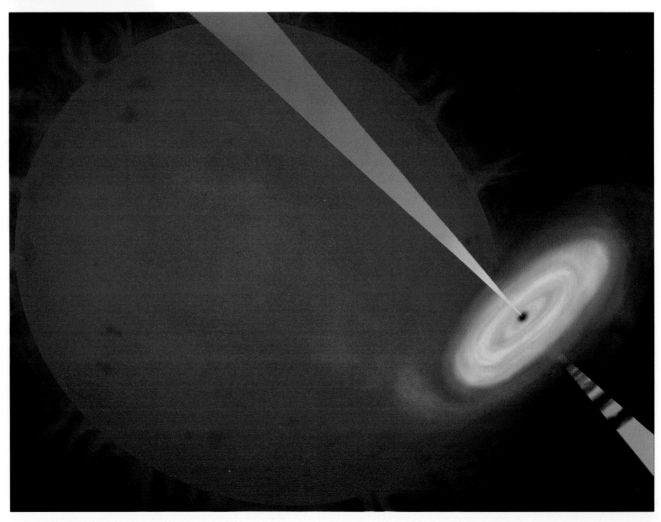

Adobe Photoshop

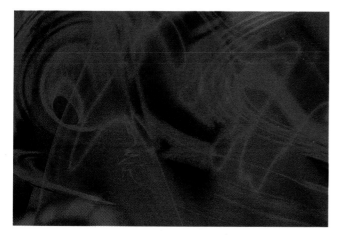

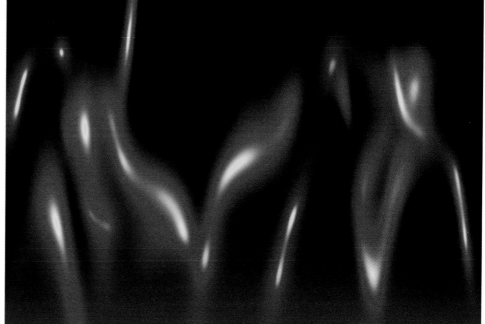

Both **7D** (above) and **Dancers** (right) are direct expressions of feelings and emotions, patterns depicting traces of human experience.

In **7D** edited textures were created using Photoshop's brushes and Distort filters. These textures were then seamlessly blended using Curves, Color Balance and Hue/Saturation controls.

Dancers was created by pasting and blending the wiggly forms. Channels and Curves were used to establish the desired densities.

Dennis Dal Covey

Adobe Photoshop,
StrataVision 3d

Cloud Samba was created in Photoshop by manipulating a still video image. The still video shots of the clouds and human figure were imported into Photoshop. An image of a single figure was copied, pasted and scaled to create three separate figures. The Wave filter (in Sine mode) was applied to the whole image to create the abstract, distorted final illustration.

➤ The limited resolution of still video can be used to your advantage. Small files allow for more experimentation, and the enlarged pixels can be used to create a textured quality that you can't easily achieve with high-resolution files.

Reclining Nude Pastel makes extensive use of Photoshop's filters and color-adjustment features. The photograph of the model was scanned and combined with a still video grab of clouds. The image was then filtered with Find Edges, and the resulting colors were inverted and adjusted with the Hue/Saturation controls to achieve the desired luminous effect.

➤ For some kinds of photo-illustrations, the resolution differences in a combination of high-resolution and low-resolution scans can be disguised and enhanced by applying filters.

At The River of Belief is a detailed fantasy-scape created with both 2D and 3D programs.

The desert plane, set of pyramids and cacti were built in StrataVision 3d. The desert floor texture map was created by scanning a photograph of water and inverting the colors in Photoshop. The photograph of the human model was also scanned and manipulated.

After these individual elements were combined in Photoshop, the snake was built in StrataVision and a sandstone texture map was applied to it. To create more realistic shadows on the snake, StrataVision's primitive solid models were used to build a basic human figure in a posture identical to that of the man in the photograph. Then directional light was positioned in the 3D program to cast shadows as they would appear in the final image.

Adobe Photoshop

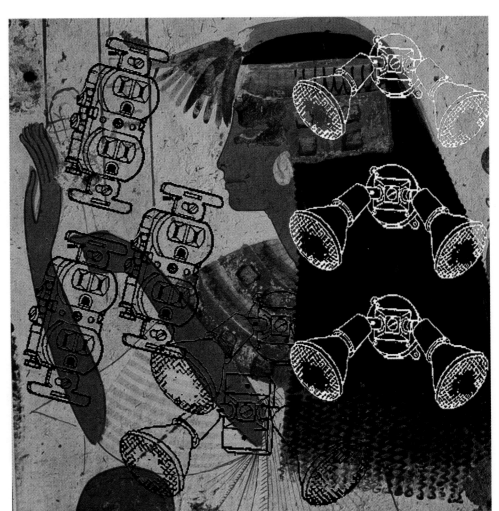

Both **How Things Change** (right) and **Office History** (above) are intended as humorous social commentary. Recent time is juxtaposed with the past, high technology with low and innocence with the modern age of nuclear capability. Icons from the past are mixed with the pervasive, superficial imagery of today. Time is compressed by the layering of images over one another in a visual "time warp."

Source images were scanned and then manipulated and montaged in Photoshop.

➤ High-quality color prints can be achieved by outputting digital files to a film recorder and then making photographic prints from the film.

**Adobe Photoshop,
Adobe Streamline,
FreeHand,
Kai's Power Tools,
Texture Synth,
Specular Collage**

Evince was created as a demo illustration for Specular Collage software.

Ink-drawn line art was scanned in, and all other elements were 3D objects. Masks were made in Photoshop's alpha channels.

The backgrounds were created in Texture Synth and then imported into Collage as elements on separate layers. Collage's Invert and Duplicate features were used on the daisy, Skew and Drop Shadow on the text and Duplicate on the main element of the frame to intensify the colors.

The head image was rendered in Photoshop, and KPT filters were applied to it to give it a 3D look. Then it was placed back into Collage, and the final illustration was rendered in Photoshop.

Flower 1 and **Flower 2** (below) are elements that were isolated from *Love at First Link-up*. Real flowers were scanned in and enhanced in Photoshop. Individual petals were duplicated and added using the clone tool, and whole layers of petals were then copied and rotated to make the flowers appear denser.

Hue, saturation and contrast were adjusted and KPT filters were applied to give them a 3D spherized look.

➤ Photoshop's feather function can be used to create more natural blends and transitions.

Love at First Link-up was created as an editorial illustration for the March, 1994 issue of *New Woman* magazine. Ink-drawings of the man and woman were scanned in as line art and converted to paths in Streamline. The other images were scanned in and saved as separate elements in Photoshop.

Each of the scanned images was treated individually in Photoshop. The clock is a scan of a real watch to which the Twirl filter and Hue/Saturation and Contrast corrections were applied. The cherub is a scanned cake decoration treated with the Gallery Effects Chrome filter. The image was smoothed with the smudge and blend tools to make it look metallic. The airplane is a small 3D metal toy scanned and manipulated with color with saturation functions.

Adobe Streamline,
Adobe Illustrator,
Adobe Photoshop,
Fractal Design Painter, JAG,
FreeHand, Infini-D

Power PC Jet began as a pencil drawing. It was scanned and then vectorized in Streamline and reproportioned in the precise PostScript illustration environment of Illustrator. Then it was rasterized in Photoshop and saved as a TIFF file.

The piece was imported into Painter and painted with the Water Color and Airbrush settings. Using a Wacom tablet helped restore the hand-drawn look to the artwork, and the watercolor paper effect was created with surface textures.

The Apple logo was rasterized in Photoshop from another Illustrator file, and the final illustration was exported as a PICT and anti-aliased in RayDream's JAG (Jaggies Are Gone) program.

Girl Version 1 is a photograph manipulated to look like a painting. To achieve the look of acrylic paints in this image, Photoshop's lasso tool was used at different feather settings, and painterly filters from Gallery Effects were applied to the selections.

➤ In an image that has been altered, the rubber-stamp tool can be used to re-establish selected parts from the original file at partial opacity to create transitions and more natural blends.

ART DIRECTOR: RICHARD SLATER

Dancing Piano is a playful piece that combines techniques from both 2D and 3D programs to create distortion and depth.

A photograph of a piano was scanned into Photoshop, where the Spherize and other Distort filters were applied. The image was saved as a TIFF file and then imported into FreeHand. The piano was built up from shapes that were traced from the TIFF template and filled with color gradients.

The background drapes started as a squiggle line created in Illustrator. It was imported into Infini-D and extruded.

The floor was drawn in perspective in Illustrator and imported into Photoshop, where the tiles were selected using the magic wand tool. A photograph of the sky from a clip-media collection (Folio, Volume 1) was pasted in at a reduced opacity to look like clouds reflected on a shiny floor.

The floor, drape and piano elements were then combined in Photoshop, and the final illustration was exported as a PICT and anti-aliased in JAG.

Adobe Photoshop,
Fractal Design Painter

Modern Odalisque, 1992
pays homage to art history as
well as to the new artistic digital
explosion. The man posing with
cat was photographed with a
video camera. Work on the image
was done in Photoshop and
Painter at low resolution to convey
the signature of the computer. The
icons framing the image were
drawn by hand.

The piece was output as a 4 x
5-inch transparency on a film
recorder, and from this a large
Cibatransparency was made. The
piece was dramatically displayed
in a state-of-the-art lightbox,
operated by remote control, to
resemble as closely as possible the
large, slim computer screen of the
near future.

➤ On Macintosh computers the
Command-Shift-3 key combination
can be used to "photograph"
whatever's on the screen and store
it as a PICT that can then be
opened for use in Photoshop or
other image-editing software.

FreeHand

A magazine spot illustration for an article on plants for balconies and decks, **Parrish** (above) uses a romantic sensibility borrowed from the look of Maxfield Parrish.

The masses of foliage were created with tight random scribbles using FreeHand's freehand tool. They were then filled with graduated green to black, duplicated, rotated and overlaid. The various flowers were also cloned, and then transformed for variety.

The vase and columns were drawn as light and shadow profiles, then filled with graduated fills to suggest highlight, core shading and reflected light. No blended shapes were necessary.

This illustration for a **Christmas Card** was created using mixtures of two Pantone colors, close-color graduated fills, and one blended shape transformation to morph flowers into doves.

The pointed leaves were placed in several layers with fill mixtures that were angled to produce depth and atmosphere. The flower shapes were created from two superimposed triple petal shapes with radial fills. One of the flowers was cloned and modified into a dove outline by dragging points and Bezier handles.

The graduated fill for the top layer of doves was set from white to white so that it would disappear as the dove developed from the flower.

The four-step blend was ungrouped and the individual parts were staggered into a graceful curve and relayered to create an ascending transition.

➤ In FreeHand, blending from an original shape to a clone of it ensures that the blend from one form to another will occur without the surprises or awkward transitional shapes that can happen if the two original shapes have different numbers of points or were not drawn with points placed in the same clockwise or counterclockwise order.

Adobe Photoshop

Cities, Houses and Desert
was created as an illustration for
the 1993 Annual Report for
ADVO, Inc.

First, the background layer of
skewed, color-filled rectangular
shapes was created in Photoshop.
Dropped shadows were added by
offsetting copies of the shapes and
saving the difference between the
original shapes and the offset ones
as selections in alpha channels;
then these selections could be
loaded and the selected areas
darkened to make the shadows.

The cities were then formed
with the pen tool. Gradation
effects were created in the interiors
of these shapes with the airbrush
and the gradient tool.

Brushes were also used in
different opacities and brush sizes
to enhance the ghosted look of the
houses. Varying opacities created
the intended layered feeling of
the artwork.

The pen tool was used to create
the Bezier curves of the highway.

➤ To eliminate banding in color
gradations, the Add Noise filter
can be applied directly to the
banded area. For the best, most
subtle results, apply the filter to
each of the individual color
channels separately.

Nightlife (left) was created for a
limited edition of Iris prints.
In Photoshop a background was
established in monotone colors,
and layers were gradually added,
including the colored border
and the overlaid linework. The
pen tool was used to create paths
that were saved as selection
boundaries so parts of the image
could be isolated and manipulated
to form the figures.

The final element, added
after the previous work was saved
as a completed background,
was the set of light beams. These
were airbrushed in Photoshop
using very broad, soft brushes;
pure white paint was applied at
varying opacities in Normal mode.

➤ To give the effect of
transparency, Photoshop's rubber
stamp tool can be used in Revert
To Saved mode in various brush
sizes to restore certain areas
to the last saved version, to make
it seem as if the eye were "seeing
through" the foreground elements.

**Adobe Photoshop,
Xaos Tools,
Andromeda Series 1,
Kai's Power Tools**

Flicker, Flash and Twirl were painted as separate Photoshop files and then combined as a triptych (the dimensions had been worked out at the outset of the project) conceived as a whimsical explanation of some of the wonders of Christmas.

Conventional pencil sketches were scanned in and painted, butterfly wings were scanned in and colorized, and a miniature decorated Christmas tree was videotaped, "grabbed" and refined using a Wacom tablet.

All the characters were done independently and saved as separate files, allowing them to make encore appearances in other forms in the future. They were individually copied and pasted into position, resized and adjusted for color balance, brightness and contrast. Before each pasted selection was dropped, it was stored as a path so the character could be selected and fine-tuned later.

The trail of stars came originally from a video grab.

Repeated copying and pasting in conjunction with the composite controls achieved the varying degrees of transparency.

The sky background and the KPT filter that created the bubbles were applied through gradation masks to achieve a gradual softening or dispersal.

When the three separate files had been completed, a canvas background color was selected from the Tru-Match color selection guide that comes with Photoshop and the files were pasted onto this colorized blank canvas, resized and positioned to achieve the triptych. The fine rule lines were drawn with the selection rectangle; the Border command was used to create a frame that was then filled with a blend.

➤ Once a special object (like a bubble or a star) is complete, save it isolated against a solid white or black background. This file can then be opened again, the object selected, feathered and pasted into the main work, where you can experiment on it with color adjustments, composite controls and filters.

Adobe Illustrator,
Adobe Photoshop,
Gallery Effects

Sleep Alarm was created with Illustrator and Photoshop. Starting from the upper left and proceeding clockwise:

The audience with 3D glasses was scanned in grayscale, composited, and colored using the Curves on each of the CMYK channels separately.

The moon was created in Illustrator, rasterized by opening in Photoshop, and composited.

The bedposts were created in Illustrator and rasterized into Photoshop, and then colorized using several graduated fills.

The sleeper was "painted" in Photoshop, working each area repeatedly with the airbrush and the Gaussian Blur.

The bedsheet was first "painted" in grays, and then a solarized copy was composited back onto the original, so the sheet retained the highlights from the original and took on the color generated by the Solarize filter.

The wood floor was created in a separate file from one rectangular plank, created by first using a graduated fill, then KPT Maximum Hue-Protected Noise, then Motion Blur, then the Gallery Effects Emboss filter. This one plank was copied and pasted repeatedly to make a flat floor, which was then pasted into the main document and distorted.

The laughing man and car crash disturbing the sleeper's dreams were first scanned from clip art and colorized in a separate file. They were then pasted, distorted, composited, copied, feathered and deleted. This sequence gives the slight halo just around the outside of the image, the halo color being the background color introduced by deleting.

The dresser, sink, hotplate and so on were painted in Photoshop in a separate file.

The vine border was a composite, cloned from a smaller segment of vine.

➤ To save space on your hard disk, make extensive use of paths, which, unlike alpha channels, can be saved with virtually no increase in file size.

➤ You don't always have to "double sample" your output halftone (lines per inch) resolution to determine the appropriate scan resolution. A ratio of 1.5:1 works just as well as 2:1 for many images, and the lower ratio means smaller files.

**Adobe Illustrator,
Adobe Streamline**

These **Illustrations** for two large-format children's books were drawn in Illustrator. The PostScript artwork could be sized to fit the format without loss of line quality or deterioration of detail. "Lines" are actually black- or white-filled shapes layered on top of color-filled objects. Textures were scanned, autotraced in Streamline and filled with color.

The **Flying West** poster was designed for the San Diego Repertory to advertise the play about the struggle and courage of two black pioneer sisters. It was produced in three Pantone colors with illustrator. The texture was original art, scanned, manipulated and placed into Illustrator to give the piece a distressed look.

Adobe Photoshop

The Unknowable Explanation was created in Photoshop and produced as a limited-edition Iris print for gallery and museum shows.

First the gradient tool was used to lay down the background (light yellow to dark brown). This was then copied, flipped and pasted. Large freeform light areas were copied with the lasso and pasted into the darker area with varying opacity settings.

Calligraphic markings were made throughout the image with the brush tool in Lighter and Darker modes and varied paint transparency. Spheres and undulations were added with three filters—Wave, Lens Flare and KPT Glass Lens.

The mask was drawn by hand in a separate file with the airbrush and smudge tools and then pasted into the background. The entire image was then reworked with the smudge tool to arrive at the final composition.

➤ With the smudge tool, the stylus or mouse takes on the characteristics of a finger running through wet oil paint. You can push and pull one color into another, model in light and dark and build up volume by mixing and blending in subtle ways. Painterly images can be worked up from a few base colors.

Angel of the Cross Being Engulfed in the Vapors of Meta-Mystical Disunion (below) is from a series of limited-edition Iris prints. The central figure was digitized with a video camera from a Renaissance painting. The head, wings and lower body were completely redrawn with Photoshop's smudge tool. The gradient tool produced the blue sky and yellow vapors. The folds in the drape were made by selecting areas, stretching, expanding and warping them with the Distort effect. These selections were repeatedly saved and applied to the image with various Opacity and Hue settings. The resulting image was then modeled into the present composition with the smudge tool.

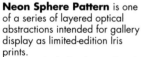

Neon Sphere Pattern is one of a series of layered optical abstractions intended for gallery display as limited-edition Iris prints.

Painter's chalk, charcoal and water color tools were used to form the underlying composition. The Gallery Effects Emboss filter was applied. Then the KPT Texture Explorer filter was used with Tile and Procedural Blend settings; this effect was then reversed with a 75% Undo. The whole procedure was repeated with a slightly different texture and an Undo setting of 50%. Next a KPT Gradient Designer Square Burst filter was applied and undone 75%. The final filter was a KPT Circular Sunburst undone to 50%. At this point the image was resampled up and worked with the smudge tool to enhance modeling and add subtleties.

Origami Self-Portrait (above) deals with flesh as cubes of folded paper. The base was a video image digitized in grayscale and then colorized with Photoshop's Hue and Saturation controls.

The resulting image was broken into squares with Painter's Glass Distortion command through the use of a large grayscale gradient square in the Paper menu. Depth was added with Photoshop's Color, Hue, Lighter and Darker brush controls to provide a base image somewhat suggestive of folded paper.

Finally, the smudge tool was used to enhance the modeling effects throughout the image and to lend a painterly appearance.

Adobe Illustrator,
Adobe Photoshop

Sketch! Poster was designed
as an illustration for a poster
promoting the Alias Sketch! 3D
design and illustration software.
It was created with the help of
Alias artist Jonathan Steinberg
using Sketch! in conjunction with
Photoshop and Illustrator. The
wasp and the flower were
created as 3D wireframe models.
Background texture was created
in Photoshop and then mapped
onto a surface created in Sketch!
Water ripples were created
from a Photoshop file of concentric
gray circles as a bump map.
Type was imported from Illustrator
and extruded.

Nurturing Knowledge is
an alternate (unpublished) version
of an editorial spot for a Pfizer
Pharmaceutical corporate
publication, illustrating the idea
that Pfizer supports emerging
local technologies around the
world. Photoshop's composite
controls were used when pasting
elements, to achieve varying
levels of opacity.

QP Doll is one of a series of postcards promoting Presslink, a printing company. The three cards illustrated the ideas of price, time and quality, the point being that you get all three with Presslink. The large letters "Q" and "P" stand for Quality Printing, and are also a pun on the word *kewpie*, as in the doll. The doll's body and hands were captured using a still video camera. The face on the doll is young Jackson Fishauf, with a small amount of Photoshop's Pinch filter applied.

**Adobe Photoshop,
Adobe Illustrator,
RayDream Designer**

Future City is a fictitious, futuristic scene built from scratch in RayDream Designer and then painted in Photoshop. Two methods of modeling—extrusion and lathing—were used to create the shapes for the buildings and flying car. The scene was composed and lighted to create angled highlights and shadows. The 3D image was then saved as a PICT and opened in Photoshop, where it was colorized and texturized.

Individual buildings were selected, converted to grayscale and imported as separate files into Illustrator, where they were used as templates to begin adding detail to the painting. Following perspective lines originally laid out in Illustrator, a series of boxes were created, copied and pasted into another Illustrator document to simulate windows. The details inside the windows were created using enlarged versions of the files to work small. The windows file was imported into Photoshop and stored in an alpha channel. The window "interiors" were cut to the clipboard from Illustrator and pasted from there into the alpha channel of the windows. When individual buildings were finished, they were pasted into the overall painting.

© Bert Monroy 1993

The New York Deli is a photorealistic recreation of a scene that actually exists, painted from a photo study—two or three photos of the overall scene and many close-ups for detail—but without any scanning.

A sketch was drawn in Illustrator, beginning with a bounding box and perspective lines. All the type was also created in Illustrator.

In Photoshop a gradient was dropped in for the background. The window area was then selected with the lasso, with the Option key held down to operate the tool in straight-line, "rubber band" mode.

The salamis hanging in the window were created with the pen tool. A gradient was inserted into the original selected shape, a highlight was applied along the edge with the airbrush tool, and the final object was cloned and modified (rotated, scaled and so on) several times.

Masks were created in three alpha channels to distinguish the building, the area in front of the window and the sidewalk. These selections were used alternately to manipulate tone and shading in distinct parts of the image. The glow in front of the window was created by lightening a selection made with a large feather radius. The reflections of doors and windows under the canopy were done with a series of filter effects (Blur, Ripple and others). For shading in the areas of the doors, windows and canopy, dark fills were used with lowered opacity. For a more realistic look, the Noise filter was applied to the whole image with a low setting of about 16.

**Adobe Photoshop,
Adobe Illustrator,
Kai's Power Tools,
Electric Image,
CyberMesh**

Army Abstract was designed as a backdrop for titles and images for an interactive presentation. A photo was scanned into Photoshop and blurred, and the Curves dialog was used to remap the colors of the photo.

Ocean Seed began with a grayscale texture created with the KPT Texture Explorer. This texture was then extruded into a 3D model with CyberMesh, a program created by John Knoll as a plug-in export filter for Photoshop. Texture maps for the floor, pillars and seed, made in Photoshop, were applied to the modeled surfaces in the Electric Image 3D program. The image was then returned to Photoshop to add the glows and other refinements.

1-bit color — a computer color system that provides only a single bit of information for each pixel in an image; this provides only two possible colors, usually black and white.

8-bit color — a computer color system that allocates 8 bits of data to describe the color of each pixel in an image; this provides 256 possible colors or levels of gray.

16-bit color — a computer color system that allocates 16 bits of data to describe the color of each pixel in an image; this provides thousands of possible colors.

24-bit color — a computer color system that allocates 24 bits of data to describe the color of each pixel in an image. Usually, the bits are allocated as 8 bits each for the three additive primary colors (red, green and blue), providing almost 16.8 million color possibilities.

32-bit color — a computer color system that allocates 32 bits of data to describe each pixel in an image; 24 bits for color information and 8 additional bits to describe transparency.

additive color mixing — producing colors by mixing colors of light rather than by mixing pigments.

antialiasing — in video and graphics, efforts to smooth the appearance of jagged lines (*jaggies*) created by the limited resolution of a graphics system. The most common antialiasing technique is to add extra dots ("phantom pixels") at random points adjacent to sloping lines or to use shading to simulate partial dots.

autotrace — a mode on some drawing programs that creates a set of vectors to represent apparent outlines of a bitmapped image; used to create vector-based images for graphics programs starting from hand-drawn artwork or a paint-style image.

Bézier — a type of curve used in some drawing programs. Bézier curves are defined by specifying anchor points that lie on the curve and control points that can be positioned to set the shape of the curve, but the control points don't necessarily lie directly on the curve itself.

bit — short for binary digit. The smallest unit of information that a computer works with. Each bit is a signal indicating *on* or *off*. Eights bits make a byte, a standard digital information unit.

bitmap — a type of graphics format where the image is made up of a large number of tiny dots (bits) arranged on a closely spaced grid. Narrowly, the term applies to 1-bit (black-and-white) graphics.

blend — 1. a feature on many graphics programs that lets you soften the edges or mix colors where two objects or regions meet. 2. a feature on object-oriented graphics programs that generates a series of intermediate steps in the transformation from one object to an object of a different shape or color.

brightness — the perceived amount of light emitted or reflected by an object.

calibration (or color calibration) — a procedure used to adjust a machine — for example, a scanner, a monitor, or a printer — to a set of manufacturer's performance standards.

cast — a tint or overemphasis of one color in a color image, particularly an unintended one. Also called *color cast*.

CD-ROM — **(for compact disk read-only memory)** an efficient, durable, inexpensive form of storage derived from the audio compact disk.

choke — a slight reduction in the size of an object's knock-out, so that the object's color can extend into the adjacent color slightly.

chroma — 1. in general, color (*hue*) information. 2. with respect to video signals, the portion of the signal that carries the color information.

chrominance — see *chroma*.

clipping path — in an object-oriented drawing program, a shape used to trim away parts of other shapes or a continuous-tone image.

CMYK — a color model based on the cyan, magenta, yellow and black inks used in color printing.

color cast — see *cast*.

color correction — the process of changing the color balance of an image to more closely approach the desired values.

color gamut — the range of colors available on a particular display or printing device.

color lookup table (CLUT) — an ordered list of active colors (or pointers to color values) for use in a graphic display, where each color in the list is selected from a much larger possible set (the *palette*). Because the lookup table is much smaller than the full color palette, it takes fewer bits to describe each color.

color management system — software that characterizes input, output and display devices in terms of the way they reproduce color and modifies the presentation of color data on the monitor so that it will be an accurate predictor of what the final color output will look like.

color matching system — a color chart, printed on paper and stored as part of a computer graphics program, that is used to specify color that will print predictably.

color model — a method for representing the color of colored items, usually by their components as specified along at least three dimensions. Common models include *RGB* (using red, green and blue light), HLS (hue, lightness and saturation), *HSV* (hue, saturation and value) and *CMYK* (using the common printing colors of cyan, magenta, yellow and black).

color separation — the process of dividing a colored image into a corresponding series of single-color images. Since process color printing is done by overprinting four single-color images, color pictures and drawings must first be made into separate images for each of these colors. Until recently, color separation was done by photographing the image through different color filters. Computerized separation systems (many of which work on the digital representation of the image rather than a photo) now make the process easier.

color space — an imaginary area or volume containing all the points whose positions represent the available colors in a system when those points are graphed on a set of axes. Color spaces are associated with companion color models, such as *HLS*, *HSV* and *RGB*.

color triangle — a diagram that shows the result of mixing a color with black (to get shades), with white (to get tints) and with gray (to get tones).

color wheel — a diagram in circular form that shows *hue* (color) as the angle around the circle.

comp — as used in graphic arts, short for *comprehensive* layout. This a mock-up of the final product made by sketching in the headlines, blocks of text, and illustrations all in the correct size and position. Some newer page layout systems can produce a sort of automated comprehensive, using blocks or wavy lines in place of the planned text.

complement — the matching color that will combine with a specified original color to make white for light, or black for pigments. In a color wheel, *complements* are diametrically opposite each other; *near complements*, or *split complements*, are a color and the tertiary colors on either side of its complement; *double complements* are two pairs of complements; a *triadic complement* is composed of three equally spaces colors; a *multiple complement* is a primary, the two secondaries on either side and the tertiaries in between.

compression — see *file compression*.

constrain — to place limits on an operation, its inputs, or the results. Drawing operations are often deliberately constrained by various options to produce selected types of lines or curves.

continuous-tone (contone) — said of an image that has shades of gray or color. Continuous-tone images cannot be reproduced in that form in most printing or digital display technologies. Instead, images with such tones must be broken up and represented by small dark and light areas or by a series of different colored dots. See also *screen*, *halftone* and *dither*.

contrast — In artwork or photographs the ratio in brightness between the lightest part of an image and the darkest part. For pictorial and graphic matter, too little contrast causes the picture to look dull or flat, while too much makes the picture seem stark and overexposed.

cool — referring to color images, ones that have a bluish tint; also called *cold*. Compare *warm*.

crop marks — in graphic arts, marks that are drawn on a photo or other piece of artwork showing which parts of the image are to be cut off before the remaining part is included in a layout. The marks are most often made in the margins, but may sometimes be made right on the image itself.

CT — an abbreviation for *continuous tone;* a graphics file format native to high-end Scitex imaging systems.

DCS — an abbrevation for *Desktop Color Separation*, a format developed for the QuarkXPress page layout program that combines four files containing high-resolution color separations of images plus a fifth file with a lower-resolution format used as a stand-in during page layout. It is now supported by many color programs and several imagesetters.

dither — to place small dots of black, white or colors in an area of an image to simulate a color that can't be represented directly because of limits on the number of colors available.

dpi — an abbreviation for *dots per inch*, a measure of the resolution of printers and other output devices.

duotone — a two-color halftone print of a black-and-white photo.

EPS or EPSF — short for *encapsulated PostScript* or *encapsulated PostScript format*, a combination of PostScript page-description language statements needed to create an image, along with an optional PICT version for quicker display. Some graphics and page layout programs may display these files on screen as boxes, while still printing the full detailed image on output.

feather — to blend or smooth the edge of a region or shape into a background or other object, especially in a slightly irregular fashion to achieve a natural-looking transition.

file compression — the process of reducing the amount of storage space occupied by a file. See also *lossy, lossless* and *JPEG*.

fill — a color or pattern occupying a defined region; to place color or pattern in a region.

filter — a software routine for altering images, packaged as a plug-in for a larger graphics program. The most common format, filters designed to work with Adobe Photoshop, are now supported widely by other graphics programs.

flatness — a measure of how much a curve is allowed to deviate from the best fit the output device (or an ideal output device) could possibly produce; expressed either in pixels or absolute distance units such as points.

flip — to reverse an image side-to-side (to flip horizontally) or top-to-bottom (to flip vertically).

four-color — used to describe printing processes that use the three subtractive primary colors (cyan, yellow and magenta) plus black to create full-color images.

GCR — an abbreviation for *gray component replacement*, the process of substituting black for the gray component that would have been created in an area of a printed image where all three process colors combine.

gradient or **graduated fill** — a feature on some graphics programs that adds a color or tint that varies smoothly from one color or brightness to another over one dimension of the area being filled.

halftone — the technique of showing shades of intensity by combining tiny full-intensity dots of varying sizes. This is the method used to reproduce tones in most kinds of printing.

hide — to temporarily remove an element of a drawing or block it from affecting the resulting image.

highlight — the lightest area on an image being photographed, and therefore the darkest area on the negative.

histogram — a chart showing the relative distribution of pixels or regions of each band of color or brightness in an image.

HSV — short for *hue, saturation* and *value*, a color model used in some graphics programs. HSV has to be translated to another model for color printing or for forming colors for display on-screen.

hue — the property of color corresponding to the frequency or wavelength of the light. This is what makes red different from green, or purple different from yellow.

imagesetter — a high-resolution output device used to set type and pictures. Most current models use a laser to write the image directly onto photosensitive film or paper.

indexed color — a color system that uses information from the image or from a program palette as a pointer to a table of output colors, rather than specifying the color directly. This is the system used in the Macintosh and Windows operating systems for 8-bit color, allowing programs to pick up to 256 colors at a time from a palette of over 16 million possibilities.

jaggies — a colloquial term for the jagged edges formed in bitmapped images' diagonal lines. See *antialiasing*.

join — the treatment of the meeting point of two or more curves or line segments; common joins include *beveled, rounded* and *mitered*.

JPEG — **1.** an acronym (pronounced jay-pegg) for *Joint Photographic Experts Group*, a committee of the International Standards Organization (ISO) that has been developing a compression standard for still images. **2.** the compression method developed by that committee.

knock-out — an area that would normally have been printed but is deliberately blocked out.

Kodak Photo CD — a scanning, compression and storage technology for recording photographs in digital format in several sizes on CD-ROM.

lightness — see *brightness*.

lossless — said of image compression that reduces file size without sacrificing any of the information in the file. For color images, lossless compression does not reduce file size as much as lossy compression.

lossy — said of image-compression techiques such as JPEG that sacrifice some of the original information in order to produce smaller files for faster processing. In most cases, the difference between the reconstructed image and the original is not visible to a casual observer.

lpi — an abbreviation for *lines per inch*, a figure used to indicate the spacing of the dot patterns making up a halftone image.

luminance — In some systems of color description, the intensity signal or brightness without the hue and saturation information.

mask — **1.** to block out part of an image, either to get rid of unwanted detail or to facilitate the addition of another image. **2.** to block out part of an image or deselect it so it won't be affected by a change or operation. **3.** a shape or region used to to block out part of an image for the above purposes.

moiré — a type of interference pattern created when two or more regularly spaced dot patterns overlap. Through proper adjustment of images and selection of patterns, moiré can be minimized.

montage — a composite image, especially one made up of elements that are distinct or would normally not be placed together.

multimedia — the combination of still images, sound and animation in a program for display on either the computer screen or a television set. Multimedia is often designed to be interactive, with input from the viewer affecting how the program proceeds.

object-oriented — as applied to graphics software, a program that describes artwork in terms of equations that define lines and shapes.

opacity — as applied to a graphic element, the degree to which an element will hide anything in layers below it.

overprint — to print a graphic element or color over another element or color.

paint — as applied to graphics programs, ones that treat images as collections of individual dots or picture elements (*pixels*) rather than as composed of distinct objects.

palette — the collection of colors or shades available to a graphics system or program. On many systems, the number of colors available for use at any time is limited to a selection from the overall system palette.

Pantone Matching System (PMS) — a system of color samples, licensed coloring materials and standards developed by Pantone, Inc. for use in specifying and checking colors for reproduction.

path — **1.** particularly in a drawing program, a combination of lines, points and curves that can be drawn in one operation without crossing a nonimage region; a path may be *open* (with two separate endpoints) or *closed* (returning to its starting point, enclosing space and thus without endpoints). **2.** in an imaging system, a route along which characters or graphic elements are placed.

PCX — a pixel-based file format used by IBM PCs and clones.

Photo CD — see *Kodak Photo CD*.

photorealistic — said of images that look like they could have been produced by a photographic process. For a computer image, this usually means one with good spatial resolution, sufficient color depth (number of colors) and accurate rendition of a real or imaginary object.

PICT — the standard file format used to pass images back and forth between Macintosh applications and the main format used by the Clipboard. A PICT file consists of collections of the Macintosh QuickDraw routines needed to create the image.

pixel — short for *picture element*, the smallest object or dot that can be changed in a display, ort a printed page or in a file.

place — to put a block of type or pictorial element at a particular position on a page.

plate — the metal, paper, or plastic sheet containing the image to be placed on the printing press. In most methods of electronic composition and layout, plates are produced from film negatives by a photographic process.

posterize — to transform an image to a more stark form by rounding tonal or color values to a small number of values.

PostScript — a trademark of Adobe Systems, Inc. for the firm's page-description language used to describe images and type in a machine-independent form.

PostScript Level 2 — an updated version of the PostScript language that adds support for color management, forms-handling, data compression and other features.

primary colors — the minimum set of colors that can be mixed to produce the full color range. For inks, the colors are cyan, magenta and yellow, while for light they are red, green and blue.

process color — color images that are created by combining four standard printing inks (cyan, magenta, yellow and black) in patterns that allow almost all colors to be represented.

PS — an abbreviation for *PostScript*, a file format used for graphics recorded in the PostScript page-description language and stored without a PICT preview. See also *EPS*.

quadtone — a four-color halftone print of a black-and-white photo.

rasterize — to change a drawing held in an object-oriented or vector (line and shape) form to the raster (collection of individual pixels) form used by most video displays and printers.

reflect — to make a mirror image of an object around a specified line.

register or registration — **1.** the alignment of the printed image with its intended position on the page. **2.** the alignment of parts of an image with other parts, especially with parts that are printed separately.

registration marks — small marks, often in the shape of crosshairs, that are used to make sure successive color plates printed on the same page line up with one another. They are usually placed outside the main image area and are trimmed off prior to binding or distribution.

render — to combine a geometric model or description of a scene with descriptions of surface characteristics and lighting to generate corresponding photorealistic images.

resolution — for graphics output, a measure of how closely packed are the spots making up an image, often measured in dots or lines per inch.

retouch — to change an image, traditionally by drawing and opaquing on the negative, or electronically by using the tools of an image-editing or painting program.

RGB — **1.** as a color model, a method of representing all colors as the combination of red, green and blue light that would create that color. **2.** as applied to video systems, short for red, green and blue, three color signals that can between them create a complete video image. Most computer graphics systems use this tri-color approach. RGB systems can be digital (each of the three signals can only assume a number of defined states) or analog (each signal can vary smoothly over its range).

rotate — to revolve an object around a specified point.

saturation — when referring to colors, the extent to which a color is made purely of a selected hue rather than a mixture of that color and its complement.

scale — to change in size, particularly to change proportionally in both dimensions.

scan — in general, to convert an image to an electronic description; particularly, to use a scanner (an input device containing a camera or photosensitive element) to produce an electronic description of the image on a sheet of paper, a piece of film, or a solid object.

scanned image — a pixel-based image produced by a scanner.

scanner — **1.** an input device that converts a photo, drawing, illustration or solid object into a corresponding electronic pixel-based image. In the graphic arts industry, sometimes called an illustration scanner. **2.** an input device that converts a page or section of printed text into the corresponding characters in memory or in a computer file; also called an *OCR (optical character recognition) scanner*.

screen — to take images that have continuous tones and break them up into patterns of tiny saturated dots, with the darker tones represented by larger or closer dots. This is a necessary step for most printing technologies, which cannot directly print intermediate tones. See also *halftone*.

screen angle — the rotation of the direction of the lines in the screen used for making halftones. In four-color process printing, the screen angles are usually set to 45 degrees for black, 75 degrees for magenta, 90 degrees for yellow and 105 degrees for cyan.

screen frequency — the number of lines or dots in a stated distance for a halftone ("screened") image; expressed as lines per inch (lpi). A 60-lpi screen is very coarse, while a 200-line screen is very fine.

secondary colors — the colors obtained by mixing two primaries in equal proportions.

select — to choose an item or a location on-screen for the next action to be carried out by a computer program.

separation — a black-and-white image representing one color component of a multicolor image. Color images must be separated into individual color components for most high-volume printing methods.

service bureau — a business that provides imagesetting and other output (and input) services to those using computers for design and production.

shade — a mixture of a hue plus black.

shading — **1.** as applied to graphic objects, the way light reflects off a surface **2.** changing the brightness and color of parts of an image to simulate depth or otherwise enhance definition.

shadow — the darkest area of a photographic image that is being photographed, and therefore the lightest area on the negative.

shear — in some drawing programs, to slant an object along a specified axis (much the way a simple type of italic might be made by slanting a normal upright roman character).

skew — see *shear*.

spot color — color that is applied only in regions where ink colors can be individually specified, rather than mixed from process colors. Compare *process color*.

spread — in color printing, a slight enlargement of an object so that it barely overlaps an adjacent object or a background color.

stochastic screening — the representation of color for printing by tiny, uniformly sized dots, placed somewhat randomly; used to avoid the moiré and softening of edges that can occur with halftone screening. Compare *halftone*.

stroke — in a drawing program or page-description language, to make a defined path part of the image by giving it visible characteristics such as line width or color.

subtractive color mixing — producing colors by combining pigments or other colorants that absorb light.

subtractive primaries — The three pigment or paint colors that can form all other colors (except pure white) when mixed together in the right ratio. For process color printing they are cyan, magenta, and yellow.

SWOP — an abbreviation for *specifications for web offset publications*, an industry standard used by most major magazines and national advertisers for color separations and color inks.

template — **1.** a document or image used to establish the format of new documents. **2.** an image used as base or guide, particularly one used to trace over.

tertiary colors — hues obtained by mixing a primary color and one of its nearest secondary colors.

TIFF — short for *tagged-image file format*, a file format developed by Aldus and Microsoft to represent pixel-based images, particularly those produced by scanners. TIFF is an open-ended standard with several variants, including *uncompressed, compressed, grayscale* and *screened* or *halftone*.

tile — **1.** to fill an area with small, regular shapes or blocks of pattern. **2.** one of the individual shapes used to fill an area.

tint — **1.** a mixture of a particular color plus white. **2.** in printing, a light or screened color applied over an area.

tonal range — the difference in brightness between the lightest and darkest colors in an image.

tone — in speaking of light and color, an intermediate between a color and gray.

toolbox — an on-screen array of icons representing tools (objects that perform operations) within a program.

transparency — for a graphic object or image, the attribute of letting an underlying image show through; transparency can be partial or total.

trap — **1.** a slight overprinting of abutting colors in printing, used to avoid gaps in the color if the printing press cannot maintain perfect registration. **2.** the extent to which a layer of ink sticks over a prior one.

tritone — a three-color halftone print of a black-and-white photo.

UCA — see *undercolor addition*.

UCR — see *undercolor removal*.

undercolor addition (UCA) — a way of compensating for the color thinning that can occur with GCR or UCR, by adding back color.

undercolor removal (UCR) — in color printing, the full or partial replacement of overprinted dark colors by black ink during the making of separations or the printing plate. This process reduces the amount of ink required and helps prevent ink trapping; see *trapping*.

value — when speaking of color or shades of gray, the degree of lightness or darkness; see *brightness*.

video frame grab — an image translated from the format used for live video, VCR or still video camera into digital format for use by computer graphics programs.

warm — referring to color images, ones that have a reddish tint. Compare *cool*.

zoom — to change the size of the area selected for viewing or display to provide either a more detailed (magnified) view or more of an overview (a reduced view). Some systems allow any amount of zoom, while others only zoom in discrete steps.